P9-DGU-134

INSIGHT GUIDES

EXPLORE

NICE

& THE FRENCH RIVIERA

CONTENTS

ARCHITECTURE FANS

There's Baroque in Vieux Nice (route 1) and Menton (route 8); Belle Époque on Nice's promenade des Anglais (route 2), in Cannes (route 11) and Monte-Carlo (route 7); and modern on Nice's promenade du Paillon (route 4).

RECOMMENDED ROUTES FOR...

CHILDREN

Antibes (route 10) and the Maures (route 14) have lovely sandy beaches, the Citadelle in St-Tropez is a hit with kids (route 13), and the colourful fish are a winner at Monaco's Musée Océanographique (route 7).

FOOD MARKETS

Succumb to the colourful fruit and vegetables at cours Saleya and St-François fish market in Vieux Nice (route 1), and the animated covered markets in Cannes (route 11), Antibes (route 10) and Menton (route 8).

GARDENERS

The Riviera's tropical vegetation is astonishing. Visit Val Rahmeh and the gardens of Menton (route 8), Villa Ephrussi de Rothschild (route 6), Domaine de Rayol (route 14) and Monaco's Jardin Exotique (route 7).

MODERN ART LOVERS

The Côte d'Azur was a hub of the 20th-century avant-garde. Visit Matisse and Chagall museums in Cimiez (route 3), the Musée Picasso in Antibes (route 10) and Matisse's chapel in Vence (route 9).

PEOPLE-WATCHING

Enjoy celeb-spotting from a terrace on the Vieux Port in St-Tropez (route 13), the obligatory stroll along La Croisette in Cannes (route 11) and the constant activity on place du Casino in Monte-Carlo (route 7).

SUPERB VIEWS

Get a bird's-eye view from the perched villages of Èze and Roquebrune (route 6), look down on Vieux Nice from the Colline du Château (route 5) and see the sea from the Corniche des Maures (route 14).

YACHTING AND SAILING

Admire the luxury craft in Antibes (route 10) and at St-Tropez (route 13), Cannes (route 11) and Monaco (route 7). Learn to sail at Bormes-les-Mimosas (route 14) and Nice's Vieux Port (route 5).

INTRODUCTION

An introduction to Nice & the French Riviera's geography, customs and culture, plus illuminating background information on cuisine, history and what to do when you're there.

The hill town of Èze, with Cap Ferrat in the distance

EXPLORE NICE

From Nice's Belle-Époque promenade des Anglais to Romanesque cathedrals and medieval hill villages, the French Riviera offers a beguiling mix of the grandiose and the intimate along with a variety of architecture waiting to be discovered.

It is the colours you notice first: stucco houses of all tones from cream via amber to deep russet; the white limestone crags of the Alpes-Maritimes against the blue of the Mediterranean Sea; and the red sandstones, grey schists, green serpentine and cork oaks of the Var. Together with the Riviera's luscious vegetation, vibrant flowers, green-grey olive trees and diverse vegetables overflowing from market stalls, these elements create a brilliant palette of hues – offset by the southern sun – which has inspired Signac, Dufy, Matisse and countless other artists over the years.

GEOGRAPHY AND LAYOUT

The routes in this guide first explore Nice (capital of the Alpes-Maritimes *département*), then they focus on the coastal strip between Menton by the Italian frontier to the east and Cannes in the west, before heading inland to Grasse and Vence in the Pre-Alp foothills, and westwards as far as St-Tropez and the rugged Massif des Maures in the neighbouring region of Var.

Town layouts

The Riviera's history and climate have largely determined the layout of its towns. Most are characterised by an Old Town in the centre, where a tight maze of medieval streets and stairways often grew up around a church or defensive keep, and tall houses and narrow streets ensured shade and relative cool even in summer.

From the 19th century, New Towns developed around them; these were characterised by neoclassical, Belle Époque and Art Deco terraces and villas, whether laid out on a grid as in Nice's New Town or romantically meandering as in Nice's Cimiez district and Cannes' Croix des Gardes.

Beyond often lies a sprawl of modern public housing estates and suburban apartment blocks and houses. The demands of both permanent residents and mass tourism have sometimes led to seemingly uncontrolled construction, where, beyond a few exclusive peninsulas, the dense *bétonisation* (concreting-up) of the coast has in places turned the Riviera from an idyllic destination into an urban nightmare of strip development.

Nice's famous promenade des Anglais

CLIMATE

A Mediterranean climate of hot dry summers, mild winters and sun that shines for more than 300 days a year has always been one of the area's attractions, although dramatic thunderstorms in late summer and in autumn, when torrential rain occasionally causes flash flooding, are not unknown. Global warming and overdevelopment have contributed to fears of rivers drying up, shortages of water and the risk of summer fires.

While the French Riviera is now principally a summer destination, Nice is a fantastic city to visit all year round. In winter or springtime, museums are less crowded, the arts season is in full swing, hotels and restaurants remain open and sunshine is still almost always guaranteed.

HISTORY AND ARCHITECTURE

Prehistoric cave dwellers, Phocaean traders, Roman garrisons and medieval monks and warlords have all left traces. However, the French Riviera's architectural heritage was largely shaped by power struggles between French-ruled Provence and the Italian-dominated Comté de Nice – which has given such an Italianate flavour to Vieux Nice – as well as battles for control of the Mediterranean between France, Spain and Italy.

The 16th and 17th centuries saw the construction of citadels at Villefranche-sur-Mer and St-Tropez and the star-shaped fortifications of Antibes. The Wars of Religion and Counter-Reformation backlash have left the area peppered with ornate Baroque churches and chapels full of starbursts, loud marble and cherubs intended to reinforce the Catholic faith. Outside Vieux Nice, the city reflects first the planning ambitions of the kings of Sardinia-Piedmont, with the elegant, classical, arcaded place Masséna and place Garibaldi, and after 1860, of its new Second-Empire French rulers, with its grid of streets, train station and the busy thoroughfare, avenue Jean Médecin.

But the area's history has also been moulded by its visitors, leaving a legacy of cheerfully eclectic Belle Époque seaside architecture evident in flouncy palatial hotels, extravagant villas, neo-Gothic Anglican churches and exotic domed Russian Orthodox churches, as well as remarkable gardens, created by the green-fingered who introduced an extraordinary array of tropical plants.

Modern innovation

If a lot of recent seaside apartment blocks are remarkably banal, clearly caring more about balconies with sea views than aesthetics or innovation, there is also some exciting modern architecture to discover, such as the Musée Chagall and along the

At the Musée d'Art Moderne et Contemporain in Nice

new promenade du Paillon in Nice, and Menton's new Cocteau museum designed by Rudy Ricciotti.

POPULATION

With a population of 344,500, Nice is France's fifth city, and lies at the heart of a conurbation of nearly 590,000 of the *département*'s 1,098,560 inhabitants. These figures reveal a vast difference between the densely populated coastal strip and sparsely inhabited interior.

Young and cosmopolitan

Despite its dowager reputation, Nice is actually a surprisingly young city. Fifty percent of its population is aged under 40, with a growing student population. Some 26,000 students are enrolled at the Université Nice Sophia Antipolis, which has a growing reputation, notably for law, social sciences and scientific research. There are also huge seasonal variations in numbers. A resort like St-Tropez swells to over 80,000 in the summer and settles back to a villagey 4,600 in winter.

The population is also distinguished by its high proportion of incomers, reflecting not just France's traditional immigration from North and West Africa, Southeast Asia, Portugal and Spain, or expat communities of Britons, Russians and Germans, but also by that from other regions of France. Italians are a large immigrant group, though they only

come from next door and feel quite at home, owning many of the properties and restaurants around Nice and Menton, a municipality that has cross-frontier administrative agreements with its neighbour Ventimiglia. Nice's most famous son is Garibaldi, founder of the Italian state, and the Italian flavour of the city is distinct.

Today, curiously, the Riviera's foreign population is not unlike its composition at the end of the 19th century, with the return of Russians and Eastern Europeans and the numerous British who have brought property in Vieux Nice, Antibes or the Grasse hinterland, although its social make-up is not necessarily the same; young Britons are often here to work and the Russians represent not old aristocracy but new fortunes.

LOCAL CUSTOMS

The influx of all these immigrants and émigrés from both France and abroad has led some to say that there has been a dilution of local culture. True, the south is capable of doing Provençal stereotypes to excess: the garish print tablecloths and dirndl skirts you will find in souvenir shops and markets have little to do with the subtlety of the original wood-block *indienne* prints, and rows of chirping pottery cicadas and olive-sprigged jugs are far from the functional spirit of true Provençal pottery. Yet the area's

Open-air fruit and vegetable markets abound

inhabitants remain firmly attached to local traditions: a game of *pétanque*; the herbs, anchovies and olives of the region's distinctive cuisine and snacks; and festivities, some of which go back for centuries. St Tropez has celebrated patron saint Torpes with the Bravades in May for over 500 years, even snooty Monaco continues to burn its boat for Saint Devota, and visit Nice or Menton at carnival time and you will find hundreds of locals participating in lively festivals that are not just put on for tourists.

DON'T LEAVE NICE & THE FRENCH RIVIERA WITHOUT...

Sipping a glass of rosé on Cours Saleya in Nice. Lined with bars and restaurants, this pedestrianised street in Vieux Nice where all life gathers is the perfect spot to enjoy the quintessential French Riviera drink. See page 29.

Taking in the views. Head to the Jardin Exotique in Èze Village, one of the French Riviera's prettiest perched villages, for uninterrupted views across the sea and coast. See page 56.

Spending an afternoon on a private beach. Make like an A-lister and rent a comfy sunbed and parasol on one of the south coast's many private beaches, such as Paloma Beach on Cap Ferrat. See page 54.

Watching the world go by from the Café de Paris in Monte-Carlo. Have a billionaire moment on the terrace of this legendary café while marvelling at the Ferraris, Lamborghinis and Bugattis driving past. See page 63.

Checking out the new Jean Cocteau museum in Menton. Opened in 2011, this striking museum exhibits works which provide a fascinating overview of the writer and filmmaker's legacy. See page 66.

Admiring the super yachts in Antibes. Head to the east side of Port Vauban and check out some of the world's biggest and most expensive private yachts, complete with on-board helicopters and submersibles. See page 75.

Strolling down La Croisette in Cannes. It's most fun during the Film Festival but with designer shops and luxury hotels on one side and the sparkling sea on the other, this famous prom is a delight at any time of year. See page 81.

Finding out about perfume in Grasse. Whether you're visiting the museum, a perfume maker or a flower grower, the world's fragrance capital is an olfactory delight. See page 85.

Wandering around the lovely market in St-Tropez. One of the best open-air markets in the area is the place to go for the finest local produce, clothes and accessories like the ubiquitous straw shopping bags. See page 91.

Heading into the 'back country'. The forests and villages of the Massif des Maures provide a striking contrast to the hustle and bustle of the coast. See page 92.

A pétanque player in action

Language

Although the official language is French, you may still hear snatches of Nissart and Provençal dialect, descended from Occitane, the ancient Low Latin language of the troubadours. Street signs in the Old Towns are often bilingual: look for the Nissart *carrièra* or Provençal *carriero* meaning *rue* or street, and *castelét* or *castela*r for château or castle.

Pétanque

Whether it is on the beach in Nice, by the river in rural Collobrières (where it now features on the primary school curriculum), under the plane trees on place des Lices in St-Tropez or the gravelly allées de la Liberté in Cannes, an enduring love of *pétanque* should dispel any doubts that you are truly in the south of France. Indeed any patch of vaguely flat land would appear ample excuse for men – it is still a largely male pastime – to get together for a game.

Derived from ancient *boules* and the *jeu provençal*, *pétanque* acquired its name *péts* or *pieds tanqués*, meaning 'feet together' (as there is no run-up and players throw the ball from within a small circle), in 1910. The use of steel rather than nailed wooden balls became established in the 1920s. One of the game's pleasures is that anyone can have a go – the Café in St-Tropez even lends balls to its customers – but tactics, throwing skills and mastering exactly the right expressions of doubt, confidence, bemusement and disbelief can take years of practice.

ECONOMY AND POLITICS

However, tourism is a major component of the southern economy, with Nice boasting the highest number of hotel beds after Paris and more than 4 million visitors a year. Cannes is also a year-round luxury tourist destination. The region's other industries include agriculture, wine and food processing, perfumes at Grasse, property development, advertising and science. Financial and banking services are important in Monaco, which smarts at being on the tax haven blacklist but continues to maintain a reputation for secrecy.

Although Nice faces many of the problems of a big modern city, such as the integration of its immigrant population and high unemployment, it is also a flourishing administrative centre and the leading congress town after Paris, thanks to France's second-largest airport; the city's 10,000 hotel rooms and the facilities offered by its Acropolis congress centre; and the emerging Arénas district near the airport.

Future plans

Meanwhile, under dynamic new mayor Christian Estrosi, Nice continues to look ahead, with plans for a second tram line and the development of the Plaine du Var as an ecological zone, comprising a

Colourful façades, Nice

Boats moored at the Cap d'Antibes

business district, football stadium and expanded port facilities, built according to the principles of sustainable develop-ment. Plans are afoot to extend the TGV line from Marseille to Nice, which is due to come into operation around 2020.

TOP TIPS

Family travel. If you are holidaying with children under 16 and want to explore the French Riviera, consider buying a Pass Isabelle Famille at the local railway station. This costs around €35 and allows two adults and two children unlimited travel for a day.

Eating out. It's usually much cheaper to go out for a meal at lunchtime as restaurants offer good-value plats du jour or two-course menus. Also, to save money, order a carafe d'eau (tap water) instead of pricey bottled water.

Free apps. The main tourist office websites have free apps of guided tours while the departmental website (www.cotedazur-tourisme.com) has free apps for local entertainment, monuments, film locations and local transport.

Getting a good deal. If you are planning on arranging your own trip, visit a price comparison website such as www.trivago.com, www.expedia.co.uk or www.kayak.co.uk to make sure you are getting the best deal on hotels, flights and car hire.

Go skiing. If you're on the French Riviera during the winter months, take the opportunity to go skiing in the Alpes de Haute Provence. You can get a direct bus from Nice train station to Isola 2000, which takes just over two hours and costs around €5 one way.

Enjoy a free tour. Greeters are a group of volunteers who offer free guided tours to visitors around particular themes, for example, architecture, food or antiques. Book at least a couple of weeks in advance at www.nice-greeters.com.

Cross the border. Menton is next to the Italian border and trains and buses on the French Riviera regularly go as far as Ventimiglia, the nearest town. The best day to visit is Friday as there is a large market on the seafront where goods are cheaper than in France.

The Côte d'Azur Card. Active families should consider buying this card which offers free access to more than 115 activities including entry to museums, fishing, vineyard visits and kayaking. It's available for three or six days and can be purchased at the local tourist office.

On the beach. Many of the French Riviera's beaches are shingle, which can be uncomfortable to sit on. Arguably the best sandy beaches are La Croisette in Cannes, Vieux Antibes and Pampelonne in Saint Tropez. Don't forget to look after your valuables.

Dining alone. Solo diners might find it difficult to be given a table in high season. Ask for a table for two and if anyone questions it when no one turns up tell them your partner can't make it. Take some reading material to keep yourself occupied.

Olives are a staple in Provençal cuisine

FOOD AND DRINK

The French Riviera's diverse fruit and vegetable produce combined with olive oil and aromatic herbs typify local dishes. However, legendary Provençal cuisine comes in a variety of styles, from hearty, age-old peasant stews to simple lightly grilled fish.

Eating out is one of the great pleasures of travelling in France, and the French Riviera has restaurants for all moods, occasions and budgets. A grand gastronomic restaurant with its white table linen, silver cloches and plethora of waiters serving elaborate preparations is very different prospect to a tiny hole-in-the-wall bistro with just one or two cooks and servers, yet each in its own way may be just as good. And at beach restaurants, which might literally have tables on the sand, the emphasis may be as much on DJs and sea views as on cuisine.

LOCAL SPECIALITIES

Olives and olive oil

Olive oil rather than butter is used for cooking and is a crucial ingredient in *anchoïade* (also known as *bagna cauda*), a warm anchovy and olive oil sauce, into which chopped raw vegetables are dipped, and *aïoli* (garlic mayonnaise), which may appear as an appetiser dip or as the ceremonial *grand aïoli* – traditionally a Friday or Christmas Eve dish – where it is served with assorted raw vegetables, cod, whelks, boiled potatoes and eggs. Black or green olives are at the base of *tapenade*, a purée of olives and capers delicious spread on toast or as an accompaniment to fish. Nice's tiny purplish-black *cailletier* olive turns up in many dishes; *à la niçoise* will often indicate a sauce made with tomatoes, onions and black olives, and may be found accompanying pasta, fish, chicken or rabbit.

Vegetable cornucopia

Superb tomatoes, courgettes of different hues and purple aubergines give Riviera cuisine its palette of colours. Preparations can be as simple as marinated red peppers – a favourite starter – or the fresh herbs and mixed young salad leaves of *mesclun*. Tomatoes appear as simple salads, chilled summer soups or as *tomates provençales*, accompanying meat and fish dishes, sprinkled with minced garlic and breadcrumbs and baked very slowly until almost caramelised. Nice's most celebrated vegetable dish is *ratatouille*, a luscious combination of tomatoes, onions, garlic, courgettes, peppers and aubergines. Look out also for *caponata*, aubergine stewed with tomatoes and capers.

You will also find all manner of vegetable *tians*, baked gratins perhaps of

Chillies and garlic at the food market on cours Saleya in Nice

courgette, squash or aubergine with egg and rice, named after the *tian* (rectangular earthenware dish) in which they are cooked. Tiny purple artichokes, almost without a choke, are braised *à la barigoule* with mushrooms and bacon, but can also be sliced very finely and eaten raw. Another treat is delicate orange-yellow courgette flowers, dipped in egg and flour and deep fried as fritters. *Blettes* (Swiss chard) is served as a vegetable or combined with apples, raisins and pine kernels in Nice's *tourte de blettes*, a surprisingly sweet tart, while stuffed cabbage, the leaves bound around a sausage meat filling, is a rustic speciality of Cannes and Grasse.

Fish

Not surprisingly given the French Riviera's glorious coastline and the trend for healthy eating, fish features heavily on the menu, especially at beach restaurants and the restaurants that line the ports in Villefranche-sur-Mer, Nice, St-Jean-Cap-Ferret and St Tropez. However, over-fishing of the Mediterranean and the decline of the Riviera's fishing fleet mean that apart from the grandest restaurants, which still buy directly from the remaining artisanal fishermen, much of the fish now comes from France's Breton and Atlantic ports. Common species include *loup* or *daurade* (sea bream), *rouget* (red mullet), *saint-pierre* (John Dory) and *thon* (tuna), as well as *seiche* or *calamar* (squid) and *poulpe* (octopus).

Sardines are a speciality in Nice, stuffed with Swiss chard, marinaded or grilled; likewise, *estocaficada* (*stockfisch* in Cannes, *stocafi* in Monaco) or salt cod, which is stewed in wine, tomatoes and olives. You will find the fish stew bouillabaisse (originally from Marseille) all along the coast, served in two courses, first the saffron-coloured soup accompanied by garlicky *rouille*, and then the fish and boiled potatoes. *Moules* (mussels), cultivated in the bay of Toulon, are very popular in the Var resorts of Bormes-les-Mimosas, Cavalaire and Le Lavandou.

Meat

Meat is not forgotten, however. This is France: almost every brasserie will have a *steak frites* on its menu, or go for succulent *daube de boeuf*, beef stewed in red wine and herbs with a touch of orange zest. Rabbit is also common, roasted with herbs or cooked *à la niçoise* with white wine, olives and tomatoes. The best lamb comes from the Alpine hinterland, while in winter you will find plenty of game in the Maures and Niçois back country.

Cheeses and desserts

The Côte d'Azur is not a major dairying or cheese-making area, but you will find some mountain-style Tomme cow's milk cheeses from the Mercantour as well as farm-produced goat's cheese *(chèvre)* from the Maures and Alpine foothills. These range from young, moist, fresh cheeses to harder, drier *crottins*. Among specialities are *poivre d'âne*, goat's cheese rolled in summer savory; tiny

Fresh fish sold for the fish stew bouillabaisse

goat's cheeses marinated in olive oil and herbs; and *brousse*, a ricotta-like fresh cheese used in dips and desserts.

Desserts are mostly based around fruit, including figs baked in tarts, gratins and crumbles, and lemon meringue tart *(tarte au citron meringuée)* made with the little lemons of Menton. Fashionable desserts include summer fruit soups and creations inspired by nostalgia for children's caramel bars and strawberry sweets.

Cuisine niçoise

Nice's distinctive cuisine is a unique fusion of Provençal and Italianate influences that come from the town's Savoyard past and its market gardening tradition. *Ratatouille* and *salade niçoise* (salad with tuna, olives, peppers, broad beans, eggs and anchovies) have travelled the world, others remain essentially local. The *pan bagnat* is like a portable snack version of *salade niçoise* in a roll. *Pissaladière* is a sort of thin, open, onion tart, garnished with anchovies and olives; the Menton variant *tarte mentonnaise* also includes tomatoes. Nice claims to have invented ravioli, but here, unlike those found in Italy, they are typically filled with leftover *daube de boeuf* and Swiss chard. Other Italianate specialities include gnocchi, made from potatoes or durum wheat, and *soupe au pistou*, a minestrone-like vegetable and bean soup into which a dollop of basil *pistou* (pesto) is stirred at the end.

Perhaps the most characteristic of all Niçois dishes is *petits farcis*, an assortment of stuffed tomatoes, aubergines, courgettes, onions and bell peppers, each with its own slightly different filling, based around variants of cooked ham, rice, herbs, minced meat and breadcrumbs, and served warm or cold.

WHERE TO EAT

As well as the elegant dining rooms of Belle Époque *grands hôtels*, family-run eateries and fashionable celebrity-chef dining destinations, there are also many Italian restaurants, especially in Monaco and Menton with their large Italian populations. A recent dining trend is the rise of wine bistros where market-inspired dishes are served with a wide choice of wines by the glass. The classic French meal consists of an *entrée* (starter), *plat* (main course) and dessert, and perhaps cheese course before dessert (and both fish and meat courses in grand restaurants). However, it is totally acceptable, especially at lunchtime, to just order an *entrée* and *plat* or *plat* and dessert.

Café-brasseries typically mutate during the course of a day, from casual

---

Food and Drink prices

Price guide for a three-course dinner for one, not including wine:

€€€€ = over 60 euros
€€€ = 40–60 euros
€€ = 25–40 euros
€ = below 25 euros

Al fresco lunch in Le Cannet

breakfast spot to full-scale restaurant at lunchtime, afternoon coffee haunt, early evening drinks rendezvous and back to restaurant in the evening. Some serve simple steaks and salads all day long, convenient when on the go. Those on the promenade des Anglais often seem best suited for breakfast, those on the port at St-Tropez are unmissable for observing yachts and passers-by at aperitif hour.

In Vieux Nice and Le Suquet in Cannes, many restaurants seem to have changed little for generations, still serving up age-old local specialities. Elsewhere, adventurous chefs, often haute-cuisine trained, are injecting new influences and creations. At such places, you might find on one hand modern experimental preparations, such as colourful purées and foamy emulsions, and fashionable presentations in glass jars; on the other hand, a return to roots – sometimes literally (think beetroot, radishes, parsnips, jerusalem artichokes and purple carrots) – and slow cooking in cast-iron casseroles.

For the best restaurants you may have to book weeks ahead; even for simpler places it's worth ringing in advance, especially in high season. It's often easier to get a table at lunch than dinner, and lunch can also be a good time to sample a top chef's style for a fraction of the dinner price.

WHAT TO DRINK

Most wine lists have a good choice of Provençal wines, including Côtes de Provence (which comes in all three colours), vast amounts of light, summery rosé, more substantial Bandol wines, and the southern Rhône appellations, such as Châteauneuf-du-Pape, Coteaux d'Aix-en-Provence and Côtes du Luberon. Something you will probably only ever see on a wine list in Nice are the rare yet fashionable Bellet wines.

The quintessential southern aperitif is pastis, made from anise and assorted plants and herbs, always diluted with water to turn a cloudy pale yellow.

Bellet Wines

Head north out of Nice towards St-Roman-de-Bellet (or take the no. 62 bus) and you come across one of France's smallest wine appellations; the only one technically cultivated entirely within a city boundary. In a tradition going back over two thousand years to the Phocaean Greeks of Nikaia, vines are planted on the precipitous narrow terraces of the Alpine foothills, with just 50ha (124 acres) of vines and just over a dozen producers, among them Château de Bellet and Domaine de la Source. High altitude and lots of wind and sunshine produce dry, fruity whites, light rosés and long-keeping spicy reds; however, Bellet's recent return to fashion and tiny scale of production means that the wines can be rather expensive. Most vineyards will receive visitors by appointment (see www.vinsdebellet.com).

Fragrant lavender

SHOPPING

As much as for sightseeing, the French Riviera is a great shopping destination, whether you are after designer fashion, the right look for the beach or regional arts and crafts.

Small individual shops and markets remain an essential part of the French lifestyle, although very touristy locations, such as St-Paul-de-Vence, have been taken over almost entirely by souvenir shops and arts-and-crafts galleries. Chic boutiques selling ultra-smart clothes and accessories at ultra-expensive prices abound in all the fashionable coastal resorts and large towns, while all along the coast you will find plenty of crafts workshops displaying a tempting array of top-quality original gifts with affordable price tags (for the most part). Sales take place in January and July and last for five weeks.

FASHION

As France's fifth city, Nice offers everything from classic French designer fashion to cheap-and-cheerful teen styles. There are several distinct shopping districts. Smart clothes and designer labels are concentrated in the New Town along avenue de Suède, avenue de Verdun and rue Paradis, and hot young designers on rue Alphonse Karr. Rue de France and rue Masséna contain more mainstream chainstores, as does avenue

Jean Médecin, home to the Centre Étoile shopping centre and practical supermarket Monoprix. Vieux Nice tends towards new-agey clothes, craft jewellery and souvenirs.

In Cannes, for diamond necklaces and *haute-couture* evening dresses suitable for walking up the steps during the Film Festival, try the prestigious boutiques clustered on boulevard de la Croisette. Younger styles, such as Zadig & Voltaire and Italian labels Missoni and Patrizia Pepe, can be found beside more mass-market chains and plenty of glitz on rue d'Antibes. Rue Meynadier, near the Marché Forville, is lined with cheaper outlets for casual wear and beachgear.

Monaco also abounds in designer labels, albeit of a more conservative bent than those in Cannes. Monaco's 'golden rectangle' is around the place du Casino, rue des Beaux Arts and the upmarket Galerie du Métropole; more boutiques can be found on avenue Princesse Grace and boulevard des Moulins.

Reflecting its starlet-and-villager dichotomy, St-Tropez's outlets range from designer labels like Dior to homegrown Atelier Rondini's Tropézienne gladiator-style sandals made since 1927

Colourful Biot glassware

Pearls for sale in Monaco

to casual yachting wear.

There are plenty of good clothes shops in Vieux Antibes, although here the style is more understated chic; think the nautical style of Blanc Bleu and handcrafted jewellery.

For the beach

Swimwear and beachgear can be a good buy all along the coast, especially at summer sale time. Most resorts have a wide range of swimsuits, sunhats and flipflops. For men and boys, true chic is St-Tropez's Villebrequin brand, with three boutiques in St-Tropez and outlets in Nice, Cannes and Monaco.

ARTS AND CRAFTS

Souvenirs run the gamut from clichéd pottery cicadas, herb mills with olive sprig motifs, and colourful Provençal print fabrics, to genuine craft pottery such as *tians* (baking dishes) and authentic basketware. Many towns, like Antibes, Bormes-les-Mimosas and Villefranche-sur-Mer, have summer craft markets that typically sell soaps, bags, pottery and jewellery. Èze has plenty of tourist tack, but you will also find attractive olive-wood bowls and chopping boards just inside the Posterne gate, and high-quality art galleries and potteries in Vieux Vence, notably on rue de l'Evêché and rue Henri Isnard. Near Antibes, Vallauris is home to countless art potteries, while Biot is known for its handblown bubble glass.

Perfumes can be a good buy in Grasse, where boutiques such as Fragonard sell their own scents and beauty products at factory prices. Look out also for the artisanal soaps and bath products made by the Savonnerie de Bormes in Bormes-les-Mimosas.

FOOD AND WINE

The Riviera abounds in tempting food shops and markets that are ideal for sampling local produce, stocking up for picnics and observing local life. Good items to take home include olive oil, table olives, olive paste and *tapenade*. The Nice area has an *appellation d'origine contrôlée* (AOC) for oil made from its *cailletier* olive. Reputable outlets include Alziari on rue St-François-de-Paule, which presses oil at its own mill, and Oliviera on rue du Collet, both in Vieux Nice, and the 1760-built Moulin du Rossignol in Grasse. You can usually taste before buying.

For sweet treats, go for chocolates, candied fruit and other gourmet items from Maison Auer in Vieux-Nice, candied fruits and violet- and rose- flavoured lollipops, chocolates and jams from Confiserie Florian by Nice's Vieux Port, and at Pont du Loup between Vence and Grasse. Marrons glacés from Collobrières in the Massif des Maures are another local speciality.

Other regional produce includes Côtes de Provence wines produced on the Cap Brégançon and St-Tropez peninsula, Bellet wines (see page 17), pastis and local aperitifs such as *vin d'oranger* and *pêche de vigne*.

Fast cars at the Casino de Monte-Carlo

ENTERTAINMENT

The French Riviera's nightclubs and casinos are all part of the south of France's hedonist image, but there are plenty of cultural attractions to suit more highbrow tastes as well.

Between them, Nice, Cannes, St-Tropez and Monte-Carlo offer a comprehensive all-year cultural programme, from early music to modern theatre, casinos, nightclubs and international pop. To find out what's going on, look out for free brochures in hotels and tourist offices. Other good sources are *The Riviera Times*, *The Riviera Reporter* and the cultural pages of daily newspaper *Nice Matin* available from newsstands. See page 120.

THEATRE

The leading venue for interesting modern theatre is the Théâtre National de Nice, which is dedicated to presenting contemporary drama and known for the number of new plays it premieres. Founded in 1969, the theatre moved into its premises on the promenade des Arts in 1989. Other venues in Nice include the Théâtre de la Cité, as well as offbeat fringe productions at Le Bar des Oiseaux. Also worth checking out are the small yet dynamic Antibea Théâtre in Antibes and Grasse's striking modern Théâtre de Grasse, which puts on a multidisciplinary mix of theatre, dance, music and circus by visiting companies.

DANCE

The most prestigious dance company is the Ballets de Monte-Carlo, descendant of Diaghilev's Ballets Russes. The company has regained its avant-garde reputation under choreographer Jean-Christophe Maillot, and now performs in the Grimaldi Forum (www.grimaldiforum.com) or the Casino terrace when not touring internationally. For works by visiting French and international choreographers, the biennial Cannes dance festival (www.festivaldedanse-cannes.com) is a must, while hip-hop, flamenco and contemporary dance also feature at Nice's Théâtre Lino Ventura.

ROCK AND POP

Big names of French pop and international rock perform at the Acropolis and Palais Nikaia in Nice, the Palais des Festivals in Cannes, and the Sporting d'Eté and Sporting d'Hiver in Monaco, with a smaller, more intimate setting for jazz and blues at Black Legend in Monte-Carlo (www.black-legend.com). Nice's Théâtre Lino Ventura focuses more on recent

Ballets de Monte-Carlo   *The Théâtre National de Nice*

urban and electronic music trends. There's also an active pub rock scene, mainly catering to the large Anglophone expat crowd, with bands playing venues like Ma Nolan's pub in Nice (see page 51), Monaco's La Rascasse (see page 63) and the bars of Vieux Antibes.

CLASSICAL MUSIC AND OPERA

Opulent red velvet, gilding and chandeliers are all part of the experience at the Opéra de Nice and Salle Garnier opera house in Monaco. Big gala-style opera productions are staged at Nice's Palais Nikaia, the Opéra de Nice (home of the Orchestre Philharmonique) and Monaco's Grimaldi Forum. Look out for the Ensemble Baroque de Nice (www.ensemblebaroquedenice.org), which performs in the Baroque churches and chapels of Vieux Nice and nearby towns. It aims to give authentic interpretations of 17th- and 18th-century music performed on early instruments and has a reputation for rediscovering forgotten pieces. Experimental contemporary music is the focus of the CIRM institute, which organises the Manca festival (www.cirm-manca.org) in November.

CINEMA

The Riviera itself stars in numerous films, whether it is *James Bond* at the Casino de Monte-Carlo, car chases along the Corniches or the French comedy *Brice de Nice*. With France home to the larg-est film industry in Europe, cinema-going is a major activity here, with an appetite for everything from homegrown films and Hollywood blockbusters to Middle Eastern cinema.

For non-French films, check whether they are screened in VO (*version originale* – original language with French subtitles) or VF (*version française*) dubbed into French. All year round the Cinémathèque de Nice puts on themed seasons and retrospectives. Open-air cinemas are popular in summer, such as those at Villefranche-sur-Mer and Monaco, with a different film each night in VO on a giant screen.

NIGHTLIFE

During Cannes' Film Festival, many Parisian clubs migrate south for special parties; in summer, party-goers head for Juan-les-Pins and St-Tropez, where in addition to hard-to-get-into clubs, there are also more relaxed lounge bars and a party scene on the resort's private beaches. Nice's nightlife is more centred on lounge bars and there is also a gay club scene, led by Le Glam. The Riviera is also famed for its casinos. Leading the glamour stakes are the Casino de Monte-Carlo and Croisette casinos in Cannes, while more staid casinos, dominated by slot machines, are found in Beaulieu and Menton. Spanning the discothèque-casino spectrum are La Siesta, on the beach east of Antibes, and Cannes' Palm Beach.

Menton's Fête du Citron is renowned for its colourful displays

FESTIVALS

More than anywhere else in the country, the French Riviera is a whirlwind of arts festivals over the summer season. Away from the action, even small villages have their own celebrations throughout the year.

When the main arts venues close in high summer, their place is taken by cultural events ranging from classical music and jazz festivals to electronic music parties, most of them outdoors, and films screened on the beach. All year, there's a roster of celebrations for everything from flowers to obscure saints, often with origins dating back centuries. For information on over 300 summer festivals in the region, pick up the booklet *Terre des Festivals* at tourist offices or check out www.terredesfestivals.fr. Some festivals have their own box office (online too), but tickets are also often available from tourist offices and at the branches of Fnac (www.fnac.com) in Nice, Cannes and Monte-Carlo.

CLASSICAL AND OPERA

One of the oldest cultural events on the coast is Menton's chamber music festival (www.festival-musique-menton.fr; Aug). Along with big-name ensembles and singers, there are inexpensive 6pm concerts where you can pick out the talents of the future.

Opera is the focus of Musique au Coeur (www.antibesjuanlespins.com; early July), held in the lovely gardens of Villa Eilenroc on Cap d'Antibes and Les Azuriales (www.azurialopera.com; late Aug) at the Villa Ephrussi de Rothschild on St-Jean-Cap-Ferrat.

In Cannes there are classical concerts in Les Nuits Musicales du Suquet (www.cannes-destination.fr; July), while in Monaco the acclaimed Orchestre Philharmonique de Monte-Carlo plays in the Cour d'Honneur in the palace (July–Aug).

WORLD, ROCK AND POP

Despite Menton's retirement home image, it has recently rejuvenated its arts scene with Ma Ville est Tango (www.tango-menton.com; July), four days of concerts, lessons, shows and dances. In Vence, Les Nuits du Sud (www.nuits dusud.com; mid-July–mid-Aug) sees some of the best names in world music performing in the place du Grand Jardin, with plenty of free concerts too. Meanwhile, Monte-Carlo Sporting Summer Festival (www.sportingmontecarlo.com; July and Aug) rolls out big international rock names and golden-oldie comebacks at the Sporting d'Eté on Avenue Princesse Grace.

Menton's chamber music festival is in August

JAZZ AND ELECTRONICA

Nice and Juan-les-Pins vie for the title of southern jazz capital. Jazz à Juan (www.jazzajuan.com; mid-July) held in the Pinède Gould, was founded in tribute to saxophonist Sidney Bechet, who composed *Petite Fleur* and *Dans les rues d'Antibes* when living in Antibes; while Nice Jazz Festival also includes rock and blues. Festival Pantiero, (www.festivalpantiero.com; Aug) at the Palais des Festivals is now the place for the latest electronic music trends.

THEATRE AND STAND-UP

On the hill above St-Tropez, Ramatuelle's theatre festival (www.festivalderamatuelle.com; July–Aug) puts the emphasis on one-person shows and classic comedy theatre, performed by well-known actors in a spectacular 1200-seat amphitheatre. For a more alternative scene, try the Festival du Rire (www.festival-rire.com; Sept), a week of café-théâtre and stand-up comedy at St-Raphaël.

OFF-SEASON FESTIVALS

A few big arts festivals take place over the rest of the year. As well as the celebrated Film Festival each May, Cannes' dance biennial (www.festivaldedanse-cannes.com; Nov 2015, 2017) features top dance companies from across Europe, while the Festival International du Cirque de Mon-

te-Carlo (www.montecarlofestivals.com; Jan), held under the big top in Fontvieille, is renowned as a springboard for breathtaking new circus talents.

In St-Tropez, Roman centurion Torpes is celebrated in the Bravades de St-Tropez on 16 and 17 May, while in Monaco Corsican saint Devota is remembered with a ceremonial boat burning on the eve of her fête on 26 January. The carnival tradition remains strong in the weeks leading up to Lent: the biggest event is Nice Carnaval (www.nicecarnaval.com; Feb) when spectacular giant floats parade along the promenade des Anglais, while in Villefranche-sur-Mer traditional carnival kings are replaced by a watery *bataille des fleurs* from boats in the port.

Menton's Fête du Citron has bands and floats along the seafront and spectacular sculptures made of oranges and lemons in the Jardin Biovès (www.feteducitron.com; Feb), and in late February, extravagant floats decorated with mimosa and other flowers parade around Bormes-les-Mimosas (www.bormeslesmimosas.com). In August, perfume town Grasse marks the start of the jasmine harvest with floral floats and brass bands in the Fête du Jasmin (www.ville-grasse.fr).

There are spectacular summer fireworks displays in Cannes and Monaco, while St-Raphaël's Fêtes de la Lumière (www.saint-raphael.com) celebrates Christmas with fireworks, floodlighting, street theatre and Father Christmas who arrives by boat.

King François 1er and Emperor Charles V discuss the Treaty of Nice

HISTORY: KEY DATES

Long and turbulent, the history of the Riviera saw waves of successive rulers, and traces of their presence remain today. More recently, the area's beauty, light and climate attracted artists and foreign nobility, as well as mass tourism.

FROM PREHISTORY TO THE ROMANS

400,000 BC	Prehistoric elephant hunters camp out at Terra Amata.
5thC BC	Phocaean Greeks from Marseille set up trading posts at Nikaia (Nice), Antipolis (Antibes) and Monoikos (Monaco).
2ndC BC	The Romans colonise southern France.
1stC AD	Cemenelum (Cimiez, Nice) becomes the capital of Roman province of Alpes Maritimae.

DARK AND MIDDLE AGES

5th–7thC	The barbarian invasions; Saracens establish strongholds at Èze, Ramatuelle and La Garde Freinet, but are expelled by 972.
1144	Nice becomes quasi-independent, ruled by elected consuls.
1246	Charles d'Anjou marries Béatrice de Provence and becomes Count of Provence, ruling over Anjou, Provence, Naples and Sicily.
1295	François Grimaldi, disguised as a monk, takes control of Monaco.
1388	Nice forms alliance with dukes of Savoy and declares separation from Provence under the Dédition of Nice.
1481	Cannes, Vence and the area west of the River Var (but not Nice or Monaco) become part of France. Conflicts arise between Savoy-controlled Nice and French-controlled Provence.

RENAISSANCE AND BAROQUE ERAS

1538	The Treaty of Nice is negotiated by Pope Paul III between François 1er and Emperor Charles V.
1543	The siege of Nice by French and Turkish armies.
16thC	The Wars of Religion begin: the reformist bishop is thrown out of Vence; the Counter-Reformation Baroque style dominates in Nice.

The winter season in 1920s Nice

1680–98	Antibes is fortified by Louis XIV's military architect Vauban.
1706	Louis XIV razes Nice's citadel.
1731	English visitors winter for the first time in Nice.

REVOLUTION AND EMPIRE

| 1789 | French Revolution: three years later, Revolutionary troops take Nice. |
| 1815 | Napoleon escapes from Elba and spends night in Cannes before marching on Paris via the Alps for the 'Hundred Days' in power. |

BIRTH OF TOURISM

1822	The construction of the Promenade des Anglais.
1834	Lord Henry Brougham discovers Cannes.
1860	Nice joins France after a referendum; Monaco relinquishes its rights to Menton and Roquebrune, which had also voted to join France.
1863	Monte-Carlo's casino opens.
1864	The railway reaches Nice from Paris.
1880	Guy de Maupassant discovers St-Tropez.
1890s	Queen Victoria visits Nice on several occasions.

20TH- AND 21ST-CENTURY RIVIERA

1912	The Hôtel Carlton opens in Cannes.
1922	The first 'Train Bleu' travels from Calais to the Côte d'Azur.
1923	The summer season is born when the Hôtel du Cap on the Cap d'Antibes stays open in summer for the first time.
1942–3	During World War II, the Alpes-Maritimes are occupied by Italian troops and from September 1943 by German troops.
1944	The Liberation of Provence sees landings in the Var.
1946	The first Cannes Film Festival; Picasso installs a studio in the Château Grimaldi in Antibes.
2005	Rainier III dies; Albert II is crowned sovereign prince of Monaco.
2007	Nice tramway opens.
2011	The new Jean Cocteau museum in Menton opens. Prince Albert II of Monaco marries Charlene Wittstock.
2014	The Fort de Brégançon, former official retreat of the French President near Bormes-les-Mimosas, opens to the public.

BEST ROUTES

Nice's ornate opera house

VIEUX NICE

The labyrinthine streets of Old Nice are where you can discover fine Baroque churches, funky bars and an elegant palace, as well as enjoy lots of foodie treats including the city's best ice cream.

DISTANCE: 2.5km (1.5 miles)
TIME: A full day
START: Place Masséna
END: Rue Pairolière
POINTS TO NOTE: Most churches and museums in Nice are closed at lunchtime.

Against a backdrop of pastel-coloured houses and Baroque churches and campaniles, the picturesque Old Town is a harmonious blend of old and new. It is Nice at its most traditional, where you may find elderly residents who still speak Nissart (an Occitane language related to Provençal) and restaurants serving age-old local specialities, alongside trendy cellar clubs, bohemian bars, art galleries and clothes shops which reflect the young cosmopolitan set who have rejuvenated the district. Behind the tourist-thronged main thoroughfares, there are quiet backstreets and the occasional fine doorway, carved lintel or old *lavoir* (communal wash-house) to discover.

DEVELOPMENT

Vieux Nice owes its street plan to the medieval Ville Basse (Lower Town), which grew up at the foot of the Colline du Château (Castle Hill, see page 48) in the 13th and 14th centuries. It acquired its present appearance in the 16th and 17th centuries when the population of the Ville Haute (Upper Town) was forced down from the citadel and the town was rebuilt with its Baroque churches and communal buildings.

AROUND THE OPÉRA

Begin by the *Fontaine du Soleil* in **place Masséna** and enter Vieux Nice along rue de l'Opéra. If you turn right on rue St-François-de-Paule, at no. 24 you will find the **Hôtel Beau Rivage** (see page 98), whose former guests include Nietzsche, Chekhov and Matisse. However, this route turns left, passing the **Hôtel de Ville**, which is surprisingly non-flamboyant for Nice. Opposite, at no. 14, **Alziari** (www.alziari.com) draws connoisseurs for its olive oil. Further up is the pink-col-

umned **Opéra de Nice** ❶ (see also page 120). A focal point of Nice's cultural scene, it was rebuilt in 1884 on the site of the earlier Théâtre Royal, which was gutted after a fire. At no. 7, family-run **Maison Auer** (www.maison auer.com) has been producing candied fruits and chocolates since 1820.

COURS SALEYA

The street leads into broad **cours Saleya** ❷, home to the busy **food and flower market** (Tue–Sun am; flowers all day) and **flea market** (Mon). Frequented by many of the town's best chefs, the food market's laden stalls reflect the sheer profusion and vibrant colour of the Riviera's produce. From his third-floor apartment in the big yellow house at the east end of the cours, Matisse painted those iconic pictures of the blue sea and palm trees. Bar and restaurant terraces stretch along the sides of the square and waiters do the hard sell to lure in customers, but **Le Safari**, see ❶, remains a reliable address, holding out against the chain and theme restaurants.

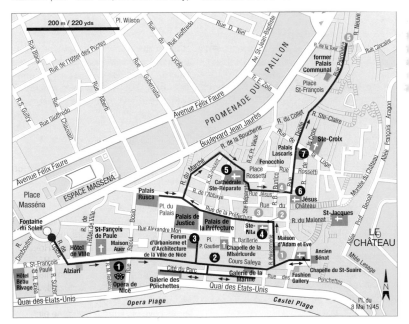

The distinctive striped awnings of the cours Saleya market

Place Pierre Gautier

Even better is the part of the market that spills into adjoining **place Pierre Gautier**. Here you are likely to be buying direct from producers, perhaps selling nothing but lemons or purple artichokes.

On the western side of the square, the **Forum d'Urbanisme et d'Architecture de la Ville de Nice** (tel: 04 97 13 31 51; Mon–Fri 8.30am–5pm, Sat 9.30am–1.30pm; free) holds exhibitions on Nice's architecture past and present. Stretching along the square's north-ern side is the **Palais de la Préfecture**, begun in the 17th century for the Dukes of Savoy, and since 1860 the *préfecture* of the Alpes-Maritimes *département*. The colonnaded façade was added when Nice was briefly returned to the kings of Sardinia-Piedmont after the Revolution.

A little further along cours Saleya is the **Chapelle de la Miséricorde** (Tue 2.30–6pm), which belongs to the Black Penitents, a religious lay fraternity, and is generally considered the finest of all Nice's Baroque interiors.

Rue des Ponchettes

Cross the cours Saleya and head through the arch to rue des Ponchettes, a double alley of low fishermen's cottages, bordered by quai des États-Unis on the other side, where the **Galerie des Ponchettes** and **Galerie de la Marine** are used for exhibitions (Tue–Sun 10am–6pm; free) put on by the municipality.

Ancien Sénat

Return to cours Saleya. At the eastern end is the pedimented building of the **Ancien Sénat**, founded in the early 17th century to administer justice on behalf of the Dukes of Savoy, who were trying to reassert their power in the quasi-independent city. Go past the adjacent Chapelle du St-Suaire (Chapel of the Holy Shroud) and take rue St-Suaire to the **Fashion Gallery**, at no. 5, which sells adventurous clothes and costume jewellery by young designers in a boutique carved into the bedrock of Castle Hill.

Route du Baroque

The reconstruction of Vieux Nice in the 1600s coincided with the Catholic Counter-Reformation, which sought a return to the faith after the schism caused by the Reformation. At the forefront was the Jesuit order founded by Ignatius Loyola, whose church of the Gesù in Rome set the model for Nice's Église du Jésus among other churches. Here, decoration takes a didactic role, and brings a new sense of theatre to church architecture to encourage popular piety, as well as an expression of the power of the church as seen by its profusion of barley-sugar columns, stripy marble, golden sunbursts and cherubs, and the 'light of God' pouring in through ceiling drums. The Route du Baroque (www.cg06.fr) pinpoints principal Baroque edifices in the Alpes-Maritimes, including Menton, Èze and Villefranche and towns inland.

Evening dining at the market

ÉGLISE STE-RITA

Return along cours Saleya and turn right into rue de la Poissonnerie. On the corner, the **Maison d'Adam et Eve**, one of the oldest buildings in the city, is decorated with a charmingly naïve 16th-century relief of Adam and Eve. Just up the street, the Église de l'Annonciation, more commonly known as **Église Ste-Rita ❹** (Mon–Sat 7am–noon and 2.30–6.30pm; Sun 8am–noon and 3–6pm; free), has an unobtrusive exterior that belies the riot of decoration inside. Daylight floods in through a half dome to reveal six side chapels with a profusion of sculpted saints, barley-sugar columns and sunbursts. This intimate gem is much loved by the Niçois, who light candles in front of the chapel of St Rita, patron saint of lost causes, to the left of the entrance.

RUE DE LA PRÉFECTURE

At the junction with rue de la Préfecture, **Les Distilleries Idéales**, see ❷, is a good place for a drink. Take a look also at the **Loggia Communale** of 1574, with its marble arcade, sheltering fragments of columns and sculpture from old buildings. This street is a characteristically Vieux Nice mix, where typically French restaurants, including the acclaimed **Bistrot Antoine**, see ❸, give way to a stretch of expat bars where you will not hear a word of French. Also of interest are old-fashioned wine merchant

Caves Caprioglio (no. 16); **Ombrelles Bestagno** (no. 17), which has been selling umbrellas and walking sticks since 1850; and **Le Palais d'Osier** (no. 3), which is crammed high with baskets.

PLACE DU PALAIS

The street borders the northern side of **place du Palais**, where the pedimented, white 19th-century **Palais de Justice** (law courts) faces the 1718 clock tower and russet-coloured façade of the Baroque **Palais Rusca**. Go through the gate to the left to see the impressive three-tiered arcades. The square, once the site of a monastery, has a **second-hand book market** on the first and third Saturday of each month.

Now head northwards along rue du Marché and rue de la Boucherie. At rue François Gallo, on the left note the **Porte Fausse**, a small stairway that once led to the River Paillon; it now contains an artwork by Sarkis (*b.*1938–) that was created for the arrival of the tramway.

PLACE DU ROSSETTI

Turn right into rue François Gallo and walk to **place du Rossetti**, the animated heart of the Old Town with flower-hung houses and café terraces.

Cathédrale Ste-Réparate

Dominating the western side is the sculpted façade of the **Cathédrale Ste-Réparate ❺** (Mon–Fri 9am–noon

Cathédrale Ste-Réparate

and 2–6pm, Sat until 7.30pm, Sun 9am–1pm and 3–6pm; free); you can just spot the multicoloured tiled dome behind the clock tower. Built on a cruciform plan inspired by St Peter's in Rome in the 1650s, it is dedicated to early Christian virgin martyr, St Réparate, the city's patron saint. Her body – accompanied by two angels (hence the name 'Baie des Anges') – is said to have arrived by boat on the shore at Nice after drifting across the Mediterranean from Palestine, where she had been decapitated at the age of 15.

The interior, which has preserved most of its original decor, is a grandiose if rather gloomy affair, despite the impressive painted dome over the transept, stucco decoration and a sequence of richly decorated Baroque side chapels, each of which originally belonged to a different wealthy local family or town corporation.

Queues leave no doubt, however, as to the square's biggest attraction: the ice creams and sorbets of **Fenocchio**, where over 90 flavours include coffee, rose, beer and lavender.

ÉGLISE DU JÉSUS

Leave the square to the south by rue du Jésus, crossing **place du Jésus**, the location of the popular budget eatery, **Restaurant du Jésus**, see ❹, and the Église St-Jacques or **Église du Jésus** ❻ (daily 3–6pm). It was founded by the Jesuit order in 1607 (though the present church dates from 1642–50), and with its single nave and side chapels, defined the style of Nice's Counter-Reformation Baroque churches (the blue-and-white classical façade is a later reworking). Inside, the profusion of carved and painted angels and cherubs is striking.

From the church head northwards up rue Droite, once the town's main north–south thoroughfare, and today busy with various new-agey clothes, trinket shops and art galleries.

PALAIS LASCARIS

At no. 15, a heavily bossed doorway announces the **Palais Lascaris** ❼ (tel: 04 93 62 72 40; Wed–Mon 10am–6pm; free), the 17th-century Genoese-style mansion of the Lascaris-Ventimille family and Nice's grandest secular Baroque building. The sober street façade does not prepare you for the splendour of the interior, with its magnificent vaulted stairway which is decorated with sculptures and frescoed grotesques. On the second floor, state rooms, with Baroque furniture and tapestries, have spectacular painted ceilings of the mythological scenes *Venus and Adonis*, *The Abduction of Psyche* and *The Fall of Phaeton*, where god and horses tumble from the sky amid a mass of swirling clouds. The first floor houses the municipal collection of 18th- and 19th-century musical instruments. Before leaving, take a look at the period pharmacy by the entrance, with its wooden shelves and faïence drug jars.

Buzzing place du Rossetti   *Palais Communal (on the right)*

PLACE ST-FRANÇOIS

Rue Droite runs into rue St-François and the **place St-François**, home to a small **fish market** (Tue–Sun am) around its dolphin fountain. Arcades remain from an earlier cloister, and on one side the 16th-century **Palais Communal** was the seat of town government until 1860.

Continue north along rue Pairolière, a busy shopping street, where foodie temptations include salts and spices at **Girofle et Cannelle** (no. 2) and olives at the **Maison de l'Olive** (no. 18). **L'Escalinada**, see ⑤, is a bastion of Niçois specialities, while at no. 1, customers queue up for *socca* to be eaten at rustic wooden tables at **Chez René Socca**. This quintessential Old Town snack is a sort of thin, crispy pancake made from chickpea flour and cooked in a large round iron pan. Cut into small portions, it is best served piping hot and seasoned with freshly ground black pepper.

Food and Drink

① LE SAFARI

1 cours Saleya; tel: 04 93 80 18 44; daily L and D; €€

This market-side brasserie is a Niçois institution, with a great people-watching terrace. Friendly, high-speed waiters serve up local specialities (*salade niçoise*, rabbit and artichoke salad), plus grilled meats and wood-fired pizzas.

② LES DISTILLERIES IDÉALES

24 rue de la Préfecture; tel: 04 93 62 10 66; daily 9am–midnight; €

A casual place for a drink, along the bar or crowded around tiny pavement tables.

③ BISTROT D'ANTOINE

27 rue de la Préfecture; tel: 04 93 85 29 57; Tue–Sat L and D; €€

Set amid traditional Vieux Nice bistros, this new-generation bistro has quickly made its mark. It rejuvenates regional dishes and market-inspired *plats du jour* with refined light presentation and inventive touches. There are well-chosen French regional wines too.

④ RESTAURANT DU JÉSUS

1 place du Jésus; tel: 04 93 62 26 46; Mon–Sat L and D; €

Marinated red peppers, home-made gnocchi, pizzas and *petits farcis* are among the rustic fare served at this busy budget joint, although you come here for the raucous atmosphere rather than the cuisine. No credit cards.

⑤ L'ESCALINADA

22 rue Paroilière; tel: 04 93 62 11 71; daily L and D; €€

This Vieux Nice shrine to traditional Niçois specialities is always packed. Timeless recipes include sardines à *l'escabèche*, stuffed courgette flowers, gnocchi, ravioli stuffed with *daube de boeuf*, plus a very good lemon meringue tart. No credit cards.

The elegant promenade des Anglais

PROMENADE DES ANGLAIS

With its grand hotels and palm trees lining the beach, the legendary promenade des Anglais epitomises elegant Nice. Behind it, the New Town is laid out in a grid of broad avenues and garden squares and offers smart shops and a panoply of 19th- and 20th-century architecture.

> **DISTANCE:** 6km (3.75 miles)
> **TIME:** A half day
> **START/END:** Place Masséna
> **POINTS TO NOTE:** The promenade des Anglais can get very traffic clogged; all the more reason to explore on foot.

The iconic promenade skirts the Baie des Anges; to the north, modern Nice's architecture is testament to the era when it was *the* place to winter in Europe.

PLACE MASSÉNA

Nice's grandest square and psychological heart, **place Masséna** ❶ lies at the crossroads of the north–south avenue Jean Médecin and the old east–west rue de France. It symbolised the town-planning ambitions of the Consiglio d'Ornano (Council of Ornament), which was set up under the King of Sardinia-Piedmont in 1832 to mastermind the expansion of the town west of the River Paillon. A beautiful ensemble of arcaded, deep rus-

set façades, it was spruced up for the tramway in 2007, with graphic black-and-white paving and a spectacular sculpture by Jaume Plensa (see page 44). The area east of the square, promenade du Paillon, has been redeveloped with grass and walk-through fountains during recent years at a cost of €40 million, opening to the public in 2013 – but not without controversy due to its strict rules and regulations (no indecent clothing or consumption of alcohol, for example).

CARRÉ D'OR

Leave the square to the west on pedestrianised rue Masséna; it is tourist central, busy day and night with restaurants and pizzerias. Then take rue Paradis which, along with rue Masséna, avenue de Suède and avenue de Verdun, forms Nice's retail '**Carré d'Or**'. Smart clothes shops include preppy Nice-born Façonnable, Max Mara, Chanel, delectable children's clothes at Bonpoint, and designer labels and housewares at Espace Harroch.

The promenade skirts the azure-blue Baie des Anges

Turn right at the end into avenue de Verdun, past jewellers and other high-end stores to the seafront. Here, the modern Hôtel Méridien, whose rooftop bar with panoramic views is the perfect place for an aperitif in summer, and glitzy Casino Ruhl, which replaced the Belle Époque casino – still mourned by many today – in the 1970s, mark the start of the promenade des Anglais.

PROMENADE DES ANGLAIS

Sweeping westwards from Jardin Albert 1er along the Baie des Anges for 5km (3 miles), the **promenade des Anglais**, with its blue chairs, white pergolas, palm trees and grand hotels, has come to symbolise the elegance of Nice; not bad for something that began in 1822 as an employment exercise. After a harsh winter, local resident Reverend Lewis Way opened a public subscription to construct a footpath linking the Old Town to the growing British colony on the hills further west in a suburb dubbed Newborough. It gained a broad carriageway, pavement and gas lighting In the 1860s, and took on its present appearance in 1931 when the thoroughfare was widened. Despite busy traffic, it still makes a fascinating stroll with its sheer diversity of passers-by.

Palais de la Méditerranée

Just after Casino Ruhl, at no. 5, is Nice's main **Tourist Office** (see page 129). At no. 11, admire the Art Deco façade of the **Palais de la Méditerranée ❷**, built in 1929 by American millionaire Frank Jay Gould. This symbol of 1930s glamour, with its casino, theatre, art gallery, restaurant and cocktail bar, and its architecture by Charles Delmas and his son Marcel, heralded a new age of moder-

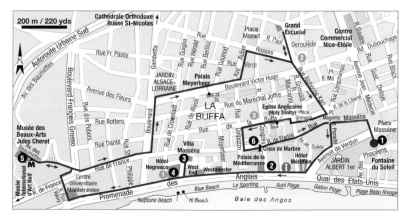

Place Masséna

nity. The Palais closed in 1978 and was shamelessly gutted, before reopening as a luxury hotel, apartments and casino.

At no. 27, the pink stucco **Hôtel Westminster** still has its grandiose reception rooms, while **Hôtel West End** (no. 31) was the first of the promenade's grand hotels and opened in 1842 as the Hôtel de Rome, welcoming many crowned heads of Europe.

Beaches

On Nice's long beach, public (free) sections alternate with private, pay beaches that are as much about image as swimming and sunbathing, although the sun loungers *(chaises longues)* are a boon on the uncomfortable pebbles. Castel Plage on quai des États-Unis at the eastern end calls itself 'the beautiful beach for beautiful people' and cultivates its arty reputation with chess matches and art shows; Beau Rivage, belonging to the elegant Vieux Nice hotel, has a vast restaurant serving Med-Asian fusion cuisine; Blue Beach in front of Hôtel West End is a chic dining address by night and child-friendly beach by day, with table tennis, a seawater pool for kids and volleyball; sporty Neptune, opposite the Negresco, has a playground, pedalos, billiards and a pontoon; while trendy Hi Beach is split into lifestyle zones – Play for families, Relax with plants and hammocks, Energy around the bar – plus computers, massages and a restaurant.

Musée Masséna

Next door, behind a luscious garden, the restored **Villa Masséna** ❸ (tel: 04 93 91 19 10; Wed–Mon 10am–6pm; free) was built in 1898 for the grandson of Maréchal Victor Masséna, one of Napoleon's generals. On the ground floor of this museum, a grandiose sequence of reception rooms and a winter garden showcase the opulent decorative style of the period, with sumptuous inlaid marquetry, panelling and gilded sphinxes. Upstairs, the collection tells the story of the aristocrats, artists and intellectuals who shaped 19th-century Nice, through an eclectic array of society portraits, paintings, documents, furniture and memorabilia. These include caricatures of Garibaldi, Napoleon's death mask, the cloak worn by Josephine for Napoleon's coronation as King of Naples and paintings of Old Nice. Among the curiosities is a poster in French and Italian calling on citizens to vote in the referendum for Nice to rejoin France on 15 and 16 April 1860. The gardens still retain some of their original plants and flowers.

The Negresco

Next to the museum, at no. 37, a sculpture of a jazz trumpeter by Niki de Saint Phalle keeps the frock-coated doormen company under the pink-and-green cupola of **Hôtel Negresco** ❹ (see page 99), Nice's grandest hotel. Built by architect Edouard Niermans, and boasting a glazed *verrière* by Gustave Eiffel over the salon, as well as lavish bath-

The iconic Hôtel Negresco

rooms and telephones in the rooms, it was one of the most modern hotels in the world when it opened in 1913. This was where F. Scott Fitzgerald stayed, and although you won't see a "diamond as big as The Ritz", you can see a crystal chandelier by Baccarat with 16,309 stones and weighing more than a tonne, designed originally for the Tsar of Russia. It is worth visiting for a meal at **Le Chantecler** (www.hotel-negresco-nice. com), which currently has two Michelin stars and 15,000 bottles in its wine cellar, or **La Rotonde**, see ➊, or simply for ogling its eccentric mix of grandeur and kitsch. Jeanne Auger, owner since 1958, chooses the decoration herself, mixing antique furniture with canopied beds, and an impressive art collection of 6,000 pieces that ranges from 18th-century portraits by Hyacinthe Rigaud to modern sculptures by Botero and de Saint Phalle.

West along the promenade

Another extravagant turreted building echos the Negresco on the next corner before the streamlined 1940s and 50s apartments of nos 43–5. At no. 63, a plaque indicates the site of Marie Bashkirtseff's Villa Aquaviva. Next door, at no. 65, the neoclassical **Centre Universitaire Méditerranéen** (www.cum-nice. org) was built in the 1930s as a centre of culture and teaching. Administered by polymath Paul Valéry, whose office has been preserved, it was the precursor of Nice University and today hosts public lectures, debates and concerts.

MUSÉE DES BEAUX-ARTS

Turn right up rue Paul Valéry and right into rue de France, passing Gloria Mansions – an icon of Art Deco Nice – at no. 125; then cross over and turn left up avenue des Beaumettes. A short cut by the steps on the left brings you out amid the fanciful villas and mock castles of Beaumettes hill, just beneath the **Musée des Beaux-Arts Jules Chéret ➎** (www. musee-beaux-arts-nice.org; Tue–Sun 10am–6pm; free), occupying the villa built for Ukrainian princess Elisabeth Kotschoubey in 1878, modelled on palaces in St Petersburg. The collection, which has works from the late Middle Ages to the early 20th century, is interesting if rather idiosyncratic, with an emphasis on artists linked to Nice and the region.

Ground floor

Paintings by the early Nice school include saints from an altarpiece by Louis Bréa. There are fine Flemish Mannerist landscapes and 18th-century French and Italian paintings, notably Fragonard's *Head of an Old Man* (undated) and Hubert Robert's *Gorges d'Ollioules* (c.1783). The biggest room is dominated by the massive *Theseus Vanquishing the Bull at Marathon* by Carle Van Loo, Nice-born court painter to Louis XV, and Louis Michel Van Loo's *Reason Conquering Force*.

First floor

Up the grand galleried staircase, where group portraits by Nicaise de Keyser

The Musée des Beaux-Arts' grand staircase

depict ancient and modern sages, the first-floor galleries focus on the late 19th and early 20th centuries. Sculpture on the landing includes a bronze of Carpeaux's *Génie de la Danse* (1822) from the Paris Opéra and an original full-scale plaster version of Rodin's *The Kiss* (1886), followed by an assemblage of Impressionist works. There are myriad pastels by Jules Chéret, a pioneering poster artist, plus Marie Bashkirtseff's wonderfully fresh self-portrait, *Autoportrait à la Palette* (1884), which was painted shortly before she died of tuberculosis in 1884 at the age of 25. A glittering figure of Nice's Russian colony, she is remembered for her journal recording high society life in Nice, the Ukraine and Paris. A small room is devoted to the strange oils and watercolours by Gustave-Adolphe Mossa, who was the museum's curator from its opening in 1928 to his death in 1971, revealing a personal, rather macabre, vision that mixes Art Nouveau curves and Symbolist angst. Another highlight is a whole room of paintings by Raoul Dufy, where a thickly painted early Fauve view of L'Estaque contrasts with the light brushstrokes and joie de vivre of later scenes of the Riviera.

In the Fabron district further west, the former villa of perfumier François Coty houses the **Musée International d'Art Naïf Anatole Jakovsky** (avenue de Fabron; tel: 04 93 71 78 33; Wed–Mon 10am–6pm; free) donated by Romanian art critic Anatole Jakovsky. He was one of the first to admire the colourful, obses-

sively meticulous works of self-taught, sometimes mentally ill, artists including Le Douanier Rousseau, Jules Lefranc and Séraphine.

BEHIND THE PROMENADE

Return down avenue des Baumettes, crossing boulevard François Grosso into rue de France. This is the workaday end of the street, with small shops and local bars; note the rare Art Nouveau façade at no. 111. At boulevard Gambetta, you can detour to the **Cathédrale Orthodoxe Russe St-Nicolas** (boulevard Tzarewitch; closed for restoration at the time of writing; charge), instantly recognisable by its onion domes, which was commissioned in 1912 by Tzarina Maria Feodorovna, mother of Tzar Nicolas II, when Nice's Russian community grew too big for an earlier church on rue Longchamp. Or turn right into boulevard Victor Hugo, a busy east–west thoroughfare with some fine architecture ranging from classical villas with wrought-iron balconies and a neo-Gothic church, to the incredibly ornate friezes of the **Palais Meyerbeer** (no. 45) and Art Deco mansion blocks.

Quartier des Musiciens
Turn left up avenue Auber in the **Quartier des Musiciens**, with its streets named after composers, which grew following the arrival of the railway in 1861. At place Mozart, turn right along rue Rossini. At the end is **Le Bistrot des Viviers**, see ❷. Two blocks north along rue Alphonse Karr

The museum's palatial villa

The museum's exquisite sculptures

is the circular façade of the **Grand Escurial** on the left; the former cinema here is now subject of controversial plans to turn it into a supermarket. Walk back down the street, past a breezy 1940s U-shaped apartment complex, to check out some adventurous fashion shops.

Rue de la Buffa

Turn right on rue de la Liberté, crossing place Grimaldi to rue de la Buffa for the 1860s, neo-Gothic **Église Anglicane** (Holy Trinity Anglican Church) at no. 11.

Nearby, to the west, is restaurant **L'École de Nice**, see ❸.

Turn left down rue Dalpozzo, then back along rue de France to place Masséna. On the way, look out for the **Croix de Marbre** ❻; this discreet little shrine, with its cross under a tiled dome, commemorates the meeting in 1538 between François 1er of France, Emperor Charles V and Pope Paul III. It was erected in 1568 on the site of a monastery where the Pope stayed when he was refused accommodation by the inhabitants of Vieux Nice.

Food and Drink

❶ LA ROTONDE

Hôtel Negresco, 37 promenade des Anglais; tel: 04 93 16 64 00; www.hotel-negresco-nice.com; daily 7am–10pm (until 11.30pm in July and Aug); €€

The Negresco's second restaurant is less formal than Le Chantecler but nevertheless offers elegant *cuisine niçoise* overseen by the same chef Jean-Denis Rieubland. There's a convenient all-day service in a cheerful fairground setting of merry-go-round horses and musical automatons.

❷ LE BISTROT DES VIVIERS

22 rue Alphonse Karr; tel: 04 93 16 00 48; www.les-viviers-nice.fr; Sept–July daily L and D; €€

With its classic bistro setting of mirrors and banquettes, and little brass plaques engraved with some of the showbiz names

who have dined here, the convivial annex of the elegant Les Viviers fish restaurant next door offers one of the best lunch bargains in town. Chef Jacques Rolancy, among the elite who have been recognised as a Meilleur Ouvrier de France, serves up a remarkably good-value daily lunch menu: a meat or fish choice, plus dessert. Expect a grander price à la carte, and accommodating service to all.

❸ L'ÉCOLE DE NICE

16 rue de la Buffa; tel: 04 8381 39 30; www.lecoledenice.com; Tue–Wed L, Mon–Fri D Tue–Sat; €€

This hip bistro is a partnership between Michelin-starred chef Keisuke Matsushima (see page 110) and composer/DJ Marc Panther. As well as a specially created soundtrack and artworks, the good-value menu (€25 for three courses) specialises in local dishes such as rabbit with pistou or ricotta ravioli.

Olive grove in the Parc des Arènes de Cimiez

CIMIEZ

Smart, residential Cimiez is imbued with the spirit of the Belle Époque and offers glimpses of Nice's Roman past too, but a walk here is also a must for art lovers given its superb museums dedicated to Chagall and Matisse.

DISTANCE: 3.25km (2 miles)
TIME: A half day
START: Former Majestic Hôtel, Boulevard de Cimiez
END: Monastère de Cimiez
POINTS TO NOTE: Eating options are limited, so best to start after lunch or bring a picnic. Note that the Chagall, Archaeological and Matisse museums all close on Tuesdays. The start of the route is reached from place Masséna or av. Jean Médecin via blvd Dubouchage and av. Desambrois. On the way back you can take buses nos. 15, 17 or 22 from Arènes–Musée Matisse.

The winding avenues, stucco façades and lush vegetation of Cimiez still evoke the Belle Époque when European aristocracy wintered on the Riviera.

BOULEVARD DE CIMIEZ

Begin at the bottom of **boulevard de Cimiez ❶**. Laid out in the 1880s, it threads through the district and is lined with ornate former grand hotels built when this was the most fashionable part of town. Spot the pink-and-cream former **Grand Hôtel** amid palm trees at no. 2, and next door, dating from 1908, the colossal white façade of the **Majestic**, which was once Nice's biggest hotel.

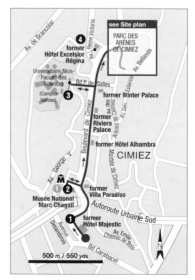

Cimiez's Église Franciscaine

Musée National Marc Chagall

Further along, at the corner with avenue Docteur Ménard, is the **Musée National Marc Chagall** ❷ (www.musee-chagall.fr; Wed–Mon May–Oct 10am–6pm, Nov–Apr until 5pm; charge), where paintings by Chagall are enhanced to great effect by the low, modern building. Inaugurated in 1973, the museum was designed in consultation with the artist by André Hermant, a pupil of Le Corbusier, specifically for the artist's paintings on Old Testament themes. In the main room, 12 paintings illustrating episodes from Genesis and Exodus reveal Chagall's ability to mix colour and narrative with a personal iconography.

A smaller side gallery holds five dream-like, rose-tinted paintings of the *Cantiques* (1957–60) on the theme of love, dedicated to his second wife Valentina Brodsky. Other works from the collection are displayed in rotation. Be sure to visit the auditorium, where there are three striking stained-glass windows and related studies depicting *The Creation of the World*. The **Café du Musée**, see ❶, is a good place for refreshments.

Grandes résidences

Return to boulevard de Cimiez, where across the street, **Villa Paradisio**, built for Baronne Hélène de Rothschild, now belongs to the town's education service, but is surrounded by a pretty public garden. Set back in gardens at no. 46, the former **Hôtel Alhambra**, with its two mosque-like minarets, and neighbouring **Villa Ellard** are two rare examples of Moorish taste. The former **Riviera Palace** at no. 39 and **Winter Palace** at no. 82 were both designed by Charles Delmas, architect of the Carlton in Cannes.

After the **Palace Prince de Galles** at no. 53, detour left along boulevard Prince de Galles to the mock medieval **gateway** ❸ of **Campus Valrose**. The neo-Gothic Château Valrose itself (main entrance on avenue de Valrose), built in 1867 for a Russian noble, is now part of Nice University and is out of bounds, but you can visit the park which sprawls over the hillside, with a waterfall, lake and an authentic Russian *isba* (house).

Grand Hotels

While earlier visitors rented or built themselves villas, by the late 19th century, when the winter season meant that being next to the sea was not that important as great views of it, hilly Cimiez's grand hotels became the place to stay; a reputation confirmed by the arrival of Queen Victoria in the 1890s. The palatial new buildings offered modern comforts, such as lifts, private bathrooms and hot running water, as well as the space to keep a retinue of servants. The crash of 1929, the birth of the summer season in the 1930s and the desire to be next to the sea sealed the decline of Cimiez's grand hotels. They closed one by one to be divided up into apartments; nevertheless, the grand Belle Époque architecture remains.

Roman excavations by the Musée d'Archéologie

Hotel Excelsior Régina

Return to boulevard de Cimiez. At the junction with avenue de la Reine Victoria, a white marble statue portrays Queen Victoria accepting flowers from figures symbolising towns on the Riviera. Crowning the boulevard behind, the ornate **Hôtel Excelsior Régina ❹** was built in 1896 in anticipation of a visit by Queen Victoria, who stayed here three times under the name of Lady Balmoral. The royal retinue occupied the entire west wing with a suite of over 70 rooms, commemorated by the crown over the entrance. The hotel was requisitioned as a military hospital during World War I and following the crash of 1929 was converted into apartments, two of which were bought by Matisse, who lived here at the end of his life, sketching on the ceiling from his bed with a brush attached to a long pole.

REMAINS OF ROMAN NICE

Across the boulevard, at the **Arènes de Cimiez ❺**, you suddenly leap back 2,000 years to the Roman city of Cemenelum, founded in the 1st century AD as a military staging post on the Via Aurelia and subsequently capital of the Imperial province of Alpes Maritimae. The amphitheatre itself is disappointing compared to the much larger, better-preserved amphitheatres at Arles, Nîmes and Fréjus, although it makes a pleasant venue for the Nice Jazz Festival in July.

Musée d'Archéologie de Nice – Site de Cimiez

You get a much better idea of the importance of Cemenelum in the adjacent **Musée d'Archéologie de Nice – Site de Cimiez ❻** (160 avenue des Arènes de Cimiez; tel: 04 93 81 59 57; Wed–Mon 10am–6pm; free) and archaeological site. Start with the museum, which has displays of statues, glassware and jewellery and sarcophagi and inscribed stelae,

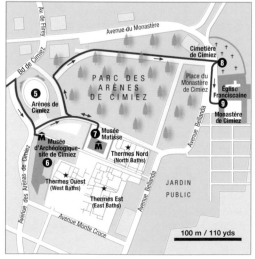

Viewing artworks at the Musée Matisse

as well as the chance to try out Roman boardgames. Exit the other side to see the extensive remains including imposing walls and bits of hypocaust from three bathing establishments dating from the settlement's 3rd-century heyday; traces of streets and shops; and a 5th-century paleo-Christian church and baptistry.

MUSÉE MATISSE

Behind the ruins, you can spot the rust-coloured **Musée Matisse ❼** (164 avenuedesArènes; www.musee-matisse-nice.org; Wed–Mon 10am–6pm; free), which is reached via the **Parc des Arènes**, a lovely grove of olive trees and a good place to picnic. The collection spans the artist's entire career, and shows how he assimilated such inspirations as Riviera sunlight, patterned textiles, classical sculpture and his voyages to North Africa and Tahiti. Highlights include Fauve portrait, small oil studies for different versions of *La Danse, Odalesque au coffret rouge* (1926), a series of small bronze heads of Jeannette, virtuoso drawing; and the 8m- (26ft-) long, cut-out *Fleurs et fruits* (1953), which provides a ripple of colour across the atrium gallery.

CIMETIÈRE DE CIMIEZ

Leave the park by the steps on the eastern side to **place du Monastère de Cimiez**, opposite the garish façade of the Franciscan church. To the left of the church enter **Cimetière de Cimiez ❽**, burial place for many British and Russian aristocrats, and follow signs to the left to pay further homage to Matisse at the simple tomb that sits on its own terrace in the gardens below. Painter Raoul Dufy is buried on the opposite side of the cemetery.

Église Franciscaine

From Dufy's tomb, follow the path through a small gate into the rose garden from where you can admire the view, including the domed **observatory** (designed by Charles Garnier and Gustave Eiffel), before visiting the early-Gothic **Église Franciscaine ❾** (Mon–Sat 10am–noon and 3–6pm; free). The draw here is the collection of three paintings – a *Pièta* triptych (c.1475), *Crucifixion* (1512) and *Deposition* (c.1520) – by Louis Bréa, the leading figure in a dynasty of Nice artists, which show his development of style.

In the adjoining **Monastère Notre-Dame de Cimiez**, a small **museum** (hours as above) presents the history of the Franciscan order in Nice.

Theatrical fountain along the promenade du Paillon

PROMENADE DU PAILLON

The landscaped promenade between Vieux Nice and the New Town is a focus for the arts and daring modern architecture, with plenty of public art to enjoy and the city's new gallery district to explore.

DISTANCE: 4km (2.5 miles)
TIME: A half day
START: Jardin Albert 1er
END: Théâtre de la Photographie et de l'Image
POINTS TO NOTE: The Mamac and Théâtre de la Photographie et de l'Image are closed Mondays; most private galleries open Tuesday to Saturday.

Running like a border between Vieux Nice and the New Town, the promenade du Paillon was created when the River Paillon was covered over for public health reasons in the 1800s. Today it has become a 'river of culture', recently redeveloped, where gardens and cultural buildings mix with outdoor sculptures.

JARDIN ALBERT 1ER

Enter the **Jardin Albert 1er** ① from avenue de Verdun. Despite busy traffic along the seafront the meandering paths, palms trees and iron bandstand still have a blowsy, pleasure-garden feel. In the centre, the **Théâtre de Verdure amphitheatre** is used for outdoor concerts in summer. Towards place Masséna, admire Bernar Venet's massive 19m- (62ft-) high painted steel *Arc 115°5* – one of a series of arcs the French sculptor has made since the 1960s that are designed according to mathematical formulae – which seems almost to float over the lawn.

PLACE MASSÉNA

Place Masséna is Nice's elegant centrepiece and, since the arrival of the tramway in 2007, is also the setting for an art installation, **Conversation à Nice** ②, by Spanish artist Jaume Plensa. Seven resin figures squatting atop tall metal poles, symbolising a dialogue between continents, are eerily white by day and illuminated from within in a subtly evolving colourful glow at night. At the same time, the **Fontaine du Soleil** ③ (Sun Fountain), with bronze sculptures by Alfred Janniot representing the planets, was returned to the southern side

The view from the Modern Art Museum (Mamac)

of the square after restoration, minus the nude statue of Apollo that crowned it when it first went up in 1956.

North of the new 'Miroir d'Eau' walk-through fountain is **Galerie Depardieu** (6 rue du Docteur Jacques Guidoni; www.galerie-depardieu.com; Mon–Sat 2.30–6.30pm), a dynamic young gallery, which mixes art shows with a programme of live jazz and readings.

PROMENADE DES ARTS

Continue along the promenade du Paillon. After Lycée Masséna on the left, make a short detour left to 8 rue Désiré Niel, where the gallery **Atclier Soardi ❹** (www.soardi.fr; Tue–Sat 10am–12.30pm and 2–6.30pm) occupies a disused film studio rented by Matisse from 1930–33 to paint his vast composition *La Danse*.

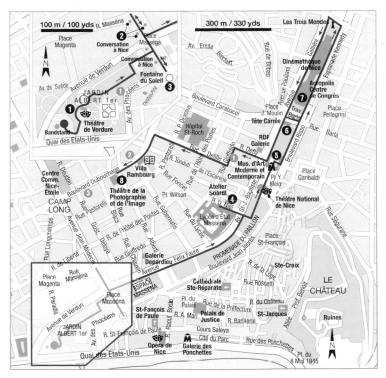

Martial Haysse's Nissa Bella, Mamac

Return to the promenade du Paillon, taking steps up onto the esplanade of the **promenade des Arts**, created in the 1980s by mayor Jacques Médecin as part of his ambitious cultural programme.

Architects Yves Bayard and Henri Vidal's carrara marble complex comprises the octagonal **Théâtre National de Nice** (see page 121), which is renowned for premiering new drama, the Mamac and the **sculpture terrace** between the two, where a *Stabile* by Calder, Borovsky's *Man with a Suitcase* and Niki de Saint Phalle's *Loch Ness Monster* fountain prepare the way for the art to come.

Mamac

While the **Musée d'Art Moderne et Contemporain** ❺ (Modern and Contemporary Art Museum, www.mamac-nice.org; Tue–Sun 10am–6pm; free) focuses on art from 1960 to the present, the museum's strength lies in its holding of the École de Nice, which is pitted against an excellent representation of parallel movements in American Pop Art, including Warhol, Lichtenstein and Johns, and abstraction by artists such as Frank Stella and Ellsworth Kelly, along with varied temporary exhibitions.

An entire room is devoted to the pivotal figure of Yves Klein, one of the leading lights of the École de Nice art movement (similar to Pop Art) which was popular in the late 1950s and 60s, who reconciled conceptual ideas and performances with a visual sensibility. This is evident in his trademark IKB (International Klein Blue) canvases and sculptures and *anthropométries*, where female models covered in paint were rolled like a living paintbrush over the canvas. Other rooms contain Arman's accumulations and cut-up musical instruments, Jacquet's *Déjeuner sur l'herbe* and an exceptional donation by Niki de Saint Phalle.

Tête Carrée

Continue north, where you cannot miss the **Tête Carrée** ❻ (Square Head) a 30m- (98ft-) high grey head that morphs into a cube (in fact the offices of the Bibliothèque Louis Nucéra, which is itself hidden underground). Sculptor Sacha Sosno describes his work as an 'inhabited sculpture' and its giant chin looks rather menacing when seen from underneath.

Palais des Congrès Acropolis

Next cross rue Barla to the **Palais des Congrès Acropolis** ❼ (1 esplanade J.F. Kennedy), a conference centre and concert hall. Although now due for a facelift, the building by Nice architects Buzzi, Bernasconi and Baptiste was considered one of the most beautiful congress centres in Europe when it opened in 1984, and integrates artworks both inside and out. By the main entrance is Arman's *Music Power*, a monumental bronze pile of sliced-up cellos.

Continue walking around the building past the bowling alley and arts cinema **Cinémathèque de Nice** (see page 120) for Noël Dolla's steel cut-out *Les trois mondes*.

Mamac artworks   *Martial Haysse's High Tension, Mamac*

GALLERY DISTRICT

Walk back towards Mamac along avenue Gallieni and turn right into rue Defly. This part of the New Town, largely undiscovered by tourists, is home to a burgeoning gallery district, where contemporary art galleries mix with antiquarian booksellers, unusual design shops and laid-back bars and bistros. On the corner, **RDF Galerie** (2 rue Defly; www.rdfgalerie. com; Tue–Sat 3–7.30pm, July and Aug by appointment) features young artists in a variety of media, from painting to video installations to collaborations with DJs

Turn left into rue Gioffredo and then right into rue Delille, perhaps stopping for a meal at **Le Gloss**, see ❶. At the end of the street turn left into boulevard Dubouchage, passing the **Villa Rambourg** (at no. 21bis), now a library of antiquarian books, posters and postcards with a lovely public garden at the rear.

Théâtre de la Photographie et de l'Image

At no. 27, behind a streamlined Moderne façade, the **Théâtre de la Photographie et de l'Image** ❽ (www.tpi-nice. org; Tue–Sun 10am–6pm; free) puts on excellent photography exhibitions in the former premises of the ornately decorated Cercle Artistique, a gentleman's club founded to promote Niçois writers and artists. There are a couple of good places to eat nearby: try **Aphrodite**, see ❷, for exciting modern cuisine, or **L'Instant T**, see ❸, for light meals.

If you want to extend the tour, continue along boulevard Dubouchage and turn right into avenue Jean Médecin for the Nice-Étoile tram stop to discover Nice's ambitious tramway art project: works by 15 international artists along 9km (6 miles) of tramway.

Food and Drink

❶ LE GLOSS

16 rue Delille; tel: 04 93 81 71 87; www.le-gloss.fr; Mon–Fri L and D; €
This sleek designer eatery is popular with laidback young Niçois for lunch or an aperitif. The easy-going menu takes in gnocchi, *farcis*, fajitas and steaks.

❷ APHRODITE

10 boulevard Dubouchage; tel: 04 93 85 63 53; www.restaurant-aphrodite.com; Tue–Sat L and D; €€€
In this dressy restaurant with a lush garden terrace, chef David Faure's beautiful, modern Mediterranean cooking is a blend of tradition and inventive touches. In the evening there is also a more revolutionary *'cuisine techno-émotionelle'* menu using modern molecular techniques.

❸ L'INSTANT T

35 boulevard Dubouchage; tel: 04 93 85 13 50; Mon–Sat 8am–7pm; €
Salads, omelettes, hamburgers and quiches are served all day at this little tea room, which has a prettily planted front garden.

Looking down from the Colline du Château

COLLINE DU CHÂTEAU AND VIEUX PORT

Now a pleasant park, the Colline du Château (Castle Hill) bears the traces of medieval Nice. It sits above the site where the Niçois' prehistoric ancestors first settled and the city's picturesque port and antiques district.

DISTANCE: 6km (3.75 miles)
TIME: A half day
START/END: Place Garibaldi
POINTS TO NOTE: The Colline du Château can also be reached by lift from the eastern end of quai des États-Unis (daily summer 8am–8pm, winter 8am–6pm; free) up to Tour Bellanda.

For centuries, the Colline du Château was the heart of medieval Nice, which grew up around the castle, before the population moved down to the coastal plain. Today, nothing remains of the cit-adelle, but the park laid out in its place is an oasis in summer with gorgeous views over the bay and the Old Town.

PLACE GARIBALDI

Start at **place Garibaldi ❶**, the beau-tiful arcaded square, built in 1782–92 by King Victor-Amédée III of Sardinia. Originally called piazza Victoria, it was later renamed after the Nice-born hero of Italian reunification, whose statue stands in the middle. On the southwest-ern side, the **Grand Café de Turin**, see ❶, is known for its seafood. Next to it, quiet rue Neuve leads into Vieux Nice. Continue along rue de la Providence to place Ste-Claire, where the **Chapelle de la Visitation ❷** has a remarkable trompe l'oeil façade.

COLLINE DU CHÂTEAU

Through the gate to the left, Escalier Ménica Rondelly zigzags up the hill-side to the **Cimetière Catholique ❸**, full of winged angels, tragic maidens and other funerary monuments. Next to it, towards the sea is the **Cimetière Israélite** (Jewish Cemetery). From here, the road climbs up to **Parc du Châ-teau ❹**, with superb views along the way. Follow the sound of water up to the **Cascade**, built in the 19th century on the site of the medieval keep, using water diverted from the River Vésubie. Steps around the rear lead to an out-door amphitheatre, used in summer for *La Castillada*, a promenade-spectacle recounting the history of Nice.

View across town to Mamac

Medieval ruins

Below, a fenced-off **archaeological site** 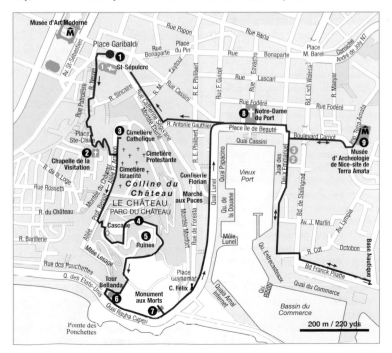 protects the fragmentary ruins of the Romanesque cathedral and bits of houses which, though poorly labelled, give some idea of the medieval residential district destroyed in the siege of 1691. Follow the path to the southwestern corner overlooking the sea to the solid round **Tour Bellanda**, a mock fortification reconstructed in the 19th century; Hector Berlioz stayed here in 1844.

You can descend by a **lift**, which occupies the well shaft dug in the 16th century to supply water to the citadelle, or by the footpath down to quai des États-Unis.

MONUMENT AUX MORTS

At the bottom turn left on quai Rauba Capeu – Nissart for 'flying hat' because of the breeze – to the powerful **Monument aux Morts**, which commemorates the 4,000 Niçois killed in World War

Boats moored in the Vieux Port

I. Elongated Modernist allegorical sculptures by Alfred Janniot of War (symbolised by figures of Liberty, Strength, Sacred Fire and Victory) face Peace (symbolised by Labour, Love of Home and Fecundity) on either side of a colonnaded temple.

VIEUX PORT

Just beyond on place Guynemar, a statue of Sardinian king Charles Félix points his finger out to sea over the **Vieux Port**, which despite its name was actually excavated only in the late 18th century (previously, fishing boats were simply pulled up on the shore and Nice's main

port was at nearby Villefranche-sur-Mer). Today, big yachts and gin palaces moor along the western quay, **quai Lunel**, while tiny wooden *pointu* fishing boats can still be seen along the eastern side.

You might want to pause at the **Marché aux Puces** (Tue–Sat 10am–6pm) on quai Lunel, source of diverse bric-a-brac and collectables. Across the street at **Confiserie Florian** (14 quai Papacino; www.confiserieflorian.com; daily 9am–noon and 2–6.30pm), you can watch chocolates being made downstairs; violet- and rose-flavour chocolates are particular specialities.

Place Ile de Beauté was constructed following Genoese fashion – with arcaded ground floor, deep-red façades and ornate trompe l'oeil window frames – along the northern side of the port in the 1780s. Halfway along, the sailors' church, **Église Notre-Dame-du-Port** ❽ (Mon–Sat 9am–noon, 3–6pm), stands out for the purity of its neoclassical style, with ribbed columns and coffered ceiling.

Musée d'Archéologie de Nice – Site de Terra Amata

Before continuing around the port, detour to 25 boulevard Carnot to the curious yet fascinating **Musée d'Archéologie de Nice – Site de Terra Amata** ❾ (entrance on Impasse Terra Amata; www.musee-terra-amata.org; Wed–Sun 10am–6pm; free). It is located at the bottom of an apartment block on the very spot, discovered in 1966, where a tribe of elephant hunters briefly camped

---

Historic Hill

For such an inconspicuous bit of rock, the Colline du Château has seen a lot of history. Settled in the 10th century BC by Ligurian tribes, Greek Nikaia grew up on its flank and during the Dark Ages the population took refuge here from barbarian invasions. By the 11th century, a keep stood on the highest point and a walled town with churches, monasteries, a market and noble residences emerged. Following the siege of Nice in 1543, Duke Emmanuel Philibert I decided to construct a powerful citadel, forcing the townspeople down to the plain. The Upper Town's fate was sealed when Nice was besieged again in 1691, and in 1706 a victorious Louis XIV razed the citadel. It was transformed into a public park in the 1820s.

The Monument aux Morts

on the beach 400,000 years ago when the sea level was 26m (85ft) higher than today. The centrepiece is a large cast of the site, showing traces of tools, animal bones and even a footprint left behind, while the upstairs mezzanine explains the lifestyle of these prehistoric nomadic hunters with displays of axeheads, flint tools and a reconstructed hut.

Boulevard Franck Pilatte

Double back to the port, where the eastern quay, **quai des Deux Emmanuels**, is lined with fish restaurants and bars, such as **Ma Nolan's**, see ②, and **L'Âne Rouge**, see ③. Take the stairs at the end up to **boulevard Franck Pilatte**, popular with locals for a promenade or for a swim from the rocks, without the crowds

of the main beaches off the promenade des Anglais. Look out for attractive twin villas Castor and Pollux on the left, and the castle-like Château d'Anglais on Mont Boron in the distance, built by English military engineer Robert Smith in 1857; and watch kids divebombing into the sea from the high board just before chic restaurant La Réserve.

ANTIQUES DISTRICT

Return to place Ile de Beauté, continuing straight on into rue Antoine Gauthier. Here, and on adjoining rue Catherine Ségurane, it is fun to browse the 100 or so **antiques dealers** clustered behind the port (www.nice-antic.com) before returning to place Garibaldi.

Food and Drink

① GRAND CAFÉ DE TURIN

5 place Garibaldi; tel: 04 93 62 29 52; daily 8am–10pm; €€

This seafood brasserie has been shucking oysters for over a century, drawing a faithful Niçois clientele despite a sometimes grouchy service. The lavish platters of *fruits de mer* include the usual suspects and some rarer treats, such as *violets* (sea potatoes) and *oursins* (sea urchins) in winter.

② MA NOLAN'S

5 quai des Deux Emmanuels; tel: 04 92 27 07 88; www.ma-nolans.com; daily L and D; €

This sophisticated Irish bar draws a French and international clientele for drinks and pub grub, either outside on the terrace or inside the woody interior where live bands play most nights. Salads, sandwiches and burgers are served all day.

③ L'ÂNE ROUGE

7 quai des Deux Emmanuels; tel: 04 93 89 49 63; www.anerougenice.com; Fri–Tue L and D, Thur D; €€€

At the dressiest of the portside restaurants, chef Michel Devillers serves up inventive starters and more classic mains, with an emphasis on fish. Service is excellent though rather formal, and there is a good-value lunch menu.

CORNICHES DRIVE

The three Corniche coast roads abound in scenic views and offer exclusive residential peninsulas, Belle Époque resorts, Roman ruins and picturesque medieval hill villages along the way.

DISTANCE: 43km (27 miles)
TIME: One day if doing a loop back to Nice; two or three days if combined with the Monaco and Menton routes
START: Vieux Port, Nice
END: Èze Village
POINTS TO NOTE: This route follows sections of all three parallel Corniche roads: the Basse (Lower) Corniche M6098, Moyenne (Middle) Corniche M6007 and Grande (Upper) Corniche M2564. The Corniches have recently been renumbered, but you may still find road signs and maps indicating the N98 and N7. Part of this tour could be done by public transport; frequent trains between Nice and Menton stop at Villefranche-sur-Mer, Beaulieu-sur-Mer and Cap d'Ail. Note that Èze station is at Èze-Bord-du-Mer and not Èze Village; similarly, the nearest station for Roquebrune Village is Carnolès, followed by a steep uphill footpath.

East towards the Italian border, the white limestone Pre-Alps fall almost directly into the sea, creating some of the Riviera's most dramatic settings and exclusive peninsulas.

BASSE CORNICHE

From place Ile de Beauté on the Vieux Port, take boulevard Carnot (M6098), start of the Basse Corniche. This climbs eastwards from Nice around the suburb of Mont Boron; the villas along it get more extravagant as you go.

Villefranche-sur-Mer

After about 5km (3 miles) the road reaches **Villefranche-sur-Mer** ❶. Although now mainly a place for a meal out for the Niçois and a stop for cruise ships, it was founded as a *ville franche* (customs free port) by the Counts of Provence. For centuries, it was the main port of the Comté de Nice – and after World War II until the 1960s, a US naval base – thanks to its natural deep-water harbour.

Turn right off the Corniche, fork left down avenue Sadi Carnot and park on place Wilson between the Citadelle and the Port de la Santé.

The breathtaking view from the Corniche above Èze

Overlooking the harbour, where a few *pointu* fishing boats still sell their catch direct, is the medieval **Chapelle St-Pierre** (tel: 04 93 76 90 70; summer Wed–Mon 10am–noon and 3–7pm, winter Wed–Mon 10am–noon and 2–6pm, closed mid-Nov–mid-Dec; charge). Often simply called the **Cocteau Chapel**, it was decorated with frescoes of the life of St Peter, patron saint of fishermen and slightly risqué images of fishing folk by poet, artist and film-maker Jean Cocteau in 1957–8. Cocteau was a frequent guest at the Hôtel Welcome next door.

Up a few steps, **place Amélie Pollonais** is home to a flea market on Sundays, a crafts market on Mondays in summer and the pleasant brasserie **Le Cosmo**, see ❶. Beyond the chapel, **quai Courbet** is lined with fish restaurants, including venerable **La Mère Germaine**, see ❷.

Go through Portail de Robert to **rue Obscure**, which runs parallel to the quayside. This atmospheric, covered street dates from the 13th century and once sheltered townsfolk when the town came under attack; it is also where Cocteau filmed part of

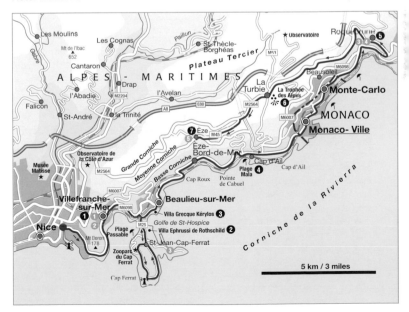

Villa Ephrussi de Rothschild

Orphée (1950). At the western end, climb stepped rue de l'Église to the 18th-century **Église St-Michel** (daily, hours vary). In front of the altar to the left of the main altar is a 17th-century wood sculpture of the Dead Christ carved from a single block of figwood; the church also has a fine organ.

Back at place Wilson, on the western side, the massive **Citadelle** (June–Sept Mon–Sat 10am–noon and 3–6.30pm, Sun 2–6.30pm, Oct–May Mon–Sat 10am–noon and 2–5.30pm, Sun 1.30–5.30pm; free) was built in 1557 by the Duke of Savoie to protect the town after the port had been occupied by Barbarossa's Turkish fleet in 1543. It now contains the Town Hall, a congress centre and four minor museums: the **Musée Volti**, with voluptuous female sculptures by Antoniucci Volti; the modern painting collection of **Musée Goetz-Boumeester**; a room devoted to the regiment of Chasseurs-Alpins; and the **Collection Roux**, displaying model scenes of medieval life.

St-Jean-Cap-Ferrat

Return to the M6098, then shortly after, take the M125 right towards St-Jean-Cap-Ferrat, a millionaires' enclave. A side road turns left to **Villa Ephrussi de Rothschild ❷** (www.villa-ephrussi.com; daily Feb–Oct 10am–6pm, July–Aug 10am–7pm, Nov–Jan Mon–Fri 2–6pm, Sat, Sun and school hols 10am–6pm; charge). The pink-and-white Italianate villa was built between 1905–12 for Béatrice Ephrussi, daughter of banker Baron Alphonse de Rothschild and wife of another wealthy banker Maurice Ephrussi, and an avid collector who filled her home with beautiful *objets*, including medieval and Rennaisance art, Gobelins tapestries, Vincennes and Sèvres porcelain and ceilings by Tiepolo. The highlight, however, is the themed gardens, complete with musical fountains, exotic cactuses, romantic roses and medieval statuary.

Return to the M125, which loops round the peninsula; soon after, to the right, a side road descends to the small but pleasant **Plage Passable**. Just beyond this turning on the right spot the

---

Walking the Caps

The best way to get to see the Riviera's exclusive headlands is along the Sentier du Littoral (Coastal Footpath). At Cap Ferrat, the path goes from the Plage Passable past the lighthouse around the end of the Cap beneath the gardens of the luxurious Grand Hôtel du Cap Ferrat to Port St-Jean. At Cap d'Ail, the path runs between Plage Mala and Plage Marquet. On Cap Martin (between Monaco and Menton) take the Sentier des Douaniers (Customs Officers' Footpath) from Roquebrune station to Carnolès via the Mangano beach and Le Corbusier's *cabanon* (cabin; tel: 04 93 35 62 87; visits by appointment); there are several places where you can bathe directly from the rocks.

gateway of **Villa les Cèdres**, the former residence of King Léopold II of Belgium. The road passes through **St-Jean-Cap-Ferrat**, which consists essentially of a yachting marina and some upmarket restaurants, as well as **Plage Paloma**, another decent small public beach on the headland east of the Port along avenue Jean Mermoz. The restaurant at private Paloma Beach, see page 112, makes for a glitzy lunch stop.

Beaulieu-sur-Mer

The M125 continues along the seafront. Once a fashionable winter resort for crowned heads, palmy **Beaulieu-sur-Mer** has a sedate feel, with its pink Belle Époque casino, yacht harbour, grand hotels and gorgeous Rotunda building. On the waterfront, the **Villa Grecque Kérylos** ❸ (impasse Gustave Eiffel; www.villa-kerylos.com; daily Feb–Oct 10am–6pm, July–Aug 10am–7pm, Nov–Jan Mon–Fri 2–6pm, Sat, Sun and school hols 10am–6pm; charge) is an idealised reconstruction of a Greek villa, inspired by 2nd-century BC villas of the island of Delos and built between 1902–8 for wealthy German scholar Theodor Reinach. It is decorated with meticulous reproductions of antique statues, frescoes, mosaics and antique furniture.

Back on the Basse Corniche, Beaulieu merges into the seaside sprawl of Èze-Bord-de-Mer, from where you can glimpse Èze Village (see page 56) high up on the cliff.

Cap d'Ail

Some 7km (4.5 miles) to the east, **Cap d'Ail** ❹ is at first sight an ungainly residential satellite for people who work in Monaco. Turn right off the main road, however, to discover Belle Époque gems, such as **Villa Lumière**, residence of the film pioneer brothers, and the **former Eden Palace hotel**, now apartments. To the right of the latter, a footpath leads down to **Plage Mala**, one of the Riviera's most beautiful beaches, with little shacks, trendy Eden restaurant and gorgeous views of the bay and mountains above.

The Basse Corniche then continues through **Monaco** (see page 58). Take the Tunnel du Serrouville through Le Rocher to Port Hercule and follow signs for Menton, climbing up along boulevard des Moulins.

GRANDE CORNICHE

At the roundabout at the end of boulevard d'Italie return to France, entering Roquebrune-Cap Martin on the D6098. Unless you are continuing on to **Menton** (see page 64), fork left onto the D6007 and left towards Roquebrune-La Turbie on the D2564, or Grande Corniche, which was laid out under Napoleon and followed the route of the Roman Via Aurelia between Rome and Spain, also known in this section as the Via Julia Augusta.

Roquebrune Village

Turn off right to **Roquebrune Village** ❺, clinging to the hillside with its square

Highly-perched Roquebrune

castle sticking up behind the orange church. Park at the foot on place Birigliano, from where steps climb up to place des Deux-Frères, with a big olive tree framed by two dramatic lumps of rock (the two brothers of its name).

Lunch in **La Grotte**, see ❸, or smarter **Les Deux Frères**, see ❹, and admire the panorama of tower-block Monaco, before exploring the tangled alleyways of old Roquebrune, some of them (such as rue Montcollet) cut into the rock itself.

At the top, the **Château** (tel: 04 93 35 07 22; call for opening times; charge) was begun in 970 and enlarged by the Grimaldis of Monaco, who ruled Roquebrune until the town made its bid for independence in 1848, joining France in 1860. In 1910 Englishman Sir William Ingram began reconstruction, leaving the castle with a vaulted guardroom and rampart walk to the town in 1926.

Take rue de la Fontaine behind the **Église Ste-Marguerite** (daily 2–5pm) and go through the gateway, where the chemin de Gorbio leads up to the cemetery. Architect Le Corbusier, whose wooden *cabanon* on Cap Martin is an icon of modern architecture and who died when bathing off the Riviera in 1965, is among those buried here. In the other direction to the cemetery, a path leads down to the **Olivier Millénaire**, a gnarled olive tree which is over a thousand years old.

La Turbie

From Roquebrune, heading west, the Grande Corniche zigzags up between olive and pine trees and limestone outcrops for 8km (5 miles) to **La Turbie**, where the white marble columns of Le Trophée des Alpes stand silhouetted against the skyline. The road leads through the edge of the village, where the **Café de la Fontaine**, see page 112, is a superb place for a meal.

Park on the square and go through one of the remaining medieval gateways and up plant-hung narrow streets to **Le Trophée des Alpes** ❻ (mid-May–mid-Sept Tue–Sun 9.30am–1pm and 2.30–6.30pm, mid-Sept–mid-May 10am–1.30pm and 2.30–5pm; charge), built around 6 BC in honour of Emperor Augustus who had subdued 45 Celto-Ligurian tribes. Subsequently sacked by barbarians and pillaged for building materials, Le Trophée is still impressive, although the statue of the emperor that once stood on top has long since gone.

MOYENNE CORNICHE

Continue along the D2564, after about 2km (miles) turn left on the D45 and then, shortly after, join the D6007. This is the Moyenne Corniche, the most direct of the three roads, which was built in the 1920s. Park below Èze Village, which is accessible only on foot.

Èze Village

Perched on top of a rocky crag at 429m (1,407ft), **Èze Village** ❼ was a prized stronghold for the Celts, Romans, Sar-

Église Ste-Marguerite, Roquebrune

acens, Guelphs and Ghibellines, before becoming a possession of the House of Savoie until 1860. Èze was largely abandoned after the 1887 earthquake, but is now a little-too-well-restored tourist destination; the gift shops and tour groups that throng the narrow streets can be almost suffocating in summer.

Enter the village through La Posterne gateway and go up rue Principale to place du Planète, turning left to the Chapelle des Pénitents Blancs and passing **Le Troubadour**, see ⑤, and the 18th-century **Église Notre-Dame-de-l'Assomption**, which has a painted dome and lashings of fake marble. At the very top of the village, the **Jardin Exotique** (see www.eze-tourisme.com for opening hours; charge), on the site of the castle razed by Louis XIV, is a feast of cactuses and succulents, and is dotted with strange terracotta statues.

Continue for about 10km (6 miles) along the D6007 to return to Nice.

Food and Drink

① LE COSMO

11 place Amélie Pollonnais, Villefranche-sur-Mer; tel: 04 93 01 84 05; daily B, L and D; €€

This friendly modern brasserie and cocktail bar has a big terrace overlooking the Cocteau Chapel and is good for inventive salads, steak tartare, pasta or catch of the day. Food is served all day in summer.

② LA MÈRE GERMAINE

9 quai Courbet, Villefranche-sur-Mer; tel: 04 93 01 71 39; www.meregermaine.com; Christmas–mid-Nov daily L and D; €€€

Run by the same family since 1938, the most famous of the string of restaurants along the harbour (Cocteau was a regular) is a dressy place, known for its fine fish and shellfish.

③ LA GROTTE

Place des Deux-Frères, Roquebrune Village; tel: 04 93 35 00 04; Thur–Tue L and D; €

A semi-troglodyte café and pizzeria with tables in the cave cut into the rock beneath the château or out on the square.

④ LES DEUX FRÈRES

Place des Deux-Frères, Roquebrune Village; tel: 04 93 28 99 00; summer Tue D, Wed–Sun L and D, winter Tue–Sat L and D, Sun D; €€

The old village school is now an attractive hotel and restaurant. Inviting, updated southern dishes might include artichoke salad or red mullet in a herb crust.

⑤ LE TROUBADOUR

Rue du Brec, Èze Village; tel: 04 93 41 19 03; mid-Dec–mid-Nov Tue–Sat L and D; €€

A long-established spot serving classic French cuisine and Provençal specialities in an old stone building in the centre of the village.

Port Hercule

MONACO

Tiny, densely populated Monaco is a curious monarchic anachronism in the midst of republican France, and packs in a fascinating mixture of architectural styles that go from royal palace to skyscraper city.

DISTANCE: 7.25km (4.5 miles)
TIME: A half day (allow a full day if visiting the palace and museums with time for lunch)
START: Place d'Armes
END: Casino de Monte-Carlo
POINTS TO NOTE: Monaco is divided into five areas, three of which are visited on this route: Monaco-Ville or Le Rocher, La Condamine around the Port Hercule and Monte-Carlo around the Casino and its seaside extension Larvotto. The principality is tiny but hilly; a useful system of lifts and escalators connects its different levels. Only cars registered in Monaco or the Alpes-Maritimes can enter Monaco-Ville, so leave your car in one of the car parks in La Condamine. Monaco train station is underground; take the avenue Prince Pierre exit for place d'Armes; the square is also served by all six of Monaco's bus routes. All sights and museums close during the Monaco Grand Prix weekend (late May) when the town is transformed by grandstands and crash barriers.

W. Somerset Maugham described it as 'a sunny place for shady people', Katherine Mansfield called it 'Real Hell', yet there is something irresistibly absurd about this tiny mini state – the second smallest in Europe after the Vatican – which is famous for its Grand Prix, billionaire residents and tax haven status,

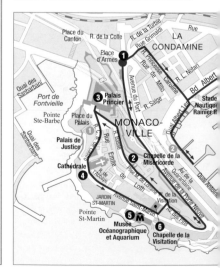

A car registration indicates Monaco's status as a principality

and ruling monarchy. Tower blocks fight for space and sea views, dwarfing the remaining Belle Époque architecture and giving Monaco the air of a mini Hong Kong on the Mediterranean.

MARCHÉ DE LA CONDAMINE

Start on the arcaded **place d'Armes ❶**, which is about as close as Monaco gets to everyday life, with its morning outdoor fruit and vegetable stalls and the covered market at one end. Butchers, *charcutiers*, pasta stalls and a couple of small bars, all with photos of Prince Albert II, reflect the omnipresence of the royal family: although nominally a constitutional monarchy, power still resides with the prince.

MONACO-VILLE

Cross over to avenue de la Porte Neuve, which climbs the side of Le Rocher to Monaco-Ville, essentially a handful of streets lined with pastel-coloured houses, which lead to the palace. The street loops via avenue des Pins to place de la Visitation (you can also get here from place d'Armes by bus route nos 1 and 2). After admiring the chocolates in the window of the **Chocolaterie de Monaco** at the end of the square, fork right into rue Princesse Marie de Lorraine and its continuation rue Basse, a nonstop parade of souvenir shops. For respite, pop into the surprisingly under-visited **Chapelle de la Miséricorde ❷**

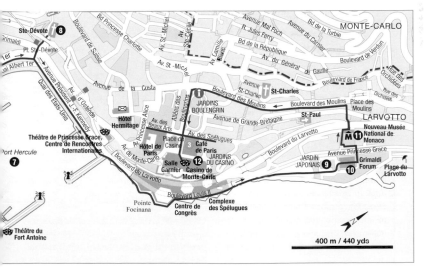

Changing of the guard, Palais Princier

(daily 10am–6pm; free), with striped marble walls, white marble sculptures and a painted wood sculpture of the Dead Christ attributed to Monaco-born François Joseph Bosio (1768–1845).

Palais Princier

The street emerges on place du Palais, where cannons and neat pyramids of cannon balls are aligned in front of the **Palais Princier** ❸ (www.palais.mc; daily July–Aug 10am–7pm, Apr–June and Sept–Oct until 6pm, closed Nov–Mar; charge), a storybook castle constructed around the fortress begun by Genoans in the 13th century. Each day, the changing of the guard takes place promptly at 11.55am, carried out by the Prince's French *carabinieri*, accompanied by much marching and drum beating. The constitution forbids the use of Monégasque guards, a precaution designed to prevent a *coup d'état*. Depending upon the season, the *carabinieri* are dressed in blue-and-red striped uniforms in winter and white uniforms in summer. The worthwhile palace audio tour includes the frescoed Galerie d'Hercule, one of the palace's Renaissance embellishments; the Galerie des Glaces, used to welcome guests during official receptions; the Cour d'Honneur, an Italianate quadrangle where Prince Albert II married Charlene Wittstock in 2011 and which hosts classical music concerts in summer; and the Salle du Trône, where he was crowned in 2005. The most appealing room is the Chambre d'York, where the Duke of York, George III's brother, died. He was on his way to visit a mistress in Genoa when he was taken ill off Monaco. Here, reported Horace Walpole, "The poor Duke of York has ended his silly, good-humoured, troublesome career in a piteous manner." Still, he managed to choose a bed chamber with a frescoed ceiling, Venetian furniture and a lovely gilt, canopied bed.

Cathédrale

Admire the views of the artificial Port de Fontvieille to the west and the original Port Hercule in the Condamine district to the east; east of here lie Monte-Carlo, a skyscraper-studded hill dubbed 'Manhattan-sur-Mer' and its man-made beach extension, Larvotto. Have a meal at **Castelroc**, see ❶, or simply take rue Colonel Bellandro de Castro, passing the Conseil National (Monaco's parliament) and the Palais de Justice (law courts) to the 19th-century **Cathédrale** ❹ (daily 8.30am–7pm, until 6pm in winter). It has a Romanesque-style façade and neo-Byzantine mosaic over the choir, and the side chapels contain saints' relics as well as an altarpiece by Louis Bréa. Around the apse are the simple slab-like royal tombs, the most recent being that of Prince Rainier II, alongside his beloved Princesse Grace.

Musée Océanographique et Aquarium

From the cathedral, avenue St-Martin leads to the **Musée Océanographique et Aquarium** ❺ (www.oceano.mc;

Café de Paris stained glass

Wealth is everywhere to see

daily Apr–June and Sept 10am–7pm, July and Aug 10am–8.30pm, Oct–Mar 10am–6pm; charge), which hugs the cliffside. Upstairs is an old-fashioned museum largely devoted to the Arctic exploration trips of 'the scientist prince', Albert I (1848–1922), which is full of specimens preserved in formaldehyde, whale skeletons and mahogany cases of navigation charts. However, the chief draw is the enormously popular aquarium downstairs, where illuminated tanks, fed by water pumped in from the sea, include a shark pit and living coral reefs populated by brightly coloured Mediterranean and tropical species.

Exit and take the steps opposite back to place de la Visitation, where the 17th-century **Chapelle de la Visitation** ❻ (tel: 377-93 50 07 00; Tue–Sun 10am–4pm; charge) provides an appropriate Baroque setting for religious paintings by Rubens, Ribera and Zurbaran.

PORT HERCULE

Meander through the gardens beneath avenue de la Porte Neuve, which are dotted with sculptures by Arman of the École de Nice (see page 46) and others, and back across place d'Armes into rue Grimaldi. Turn right down pedestrianised rue Princesse Caroline to **Port Hercule** ❼, Monaco's natural deep-water harbour ever since the Phocaeans established their trading post, Monoikos. The broad terrace along boulevard Albert 1er is a prime spot for the Grand Prix but is also used for all sorts of events, from international showjumping in June to a funfair in August; below, the outdoor swimming pool becomes an ice rink in winter.

Turn right past **La Rascasse**, see ❷, to quai Antoine 1er, for exhibitions in the

Birth of Monte-Carlo

Monaco owes its transformation from obscure olive-growing hill town to gambling capital to the Grimaldis' loss of Menton and Roquebrune in the 1860s. In search of a new source of revenue, Prince Charles III had the bright idea of opening a casino on the Spélugues hill, creating a whole new district that he modestly named after himself. After an unenthusiastic start, the prince awarded the concession to run it to businessman François Blanc, founder of the Société des Bains de Monaco (SBM). In 1864 Blanc built the Hôtel de Paris to accommodate new visitors, and in 1878 his widow Marie called in architect Charles Garnier, of Paris Opéra fame, to tack a lavish opera house onto the back of the casino to encourage gamblers to stay in town a little longer. The SBM, now majority owned by the State of Monaco, still owns most of Monte-Carlo's finest hotels, restaurants, casinos, spa, sporting facilities and nightclubs, and old-fashioned principles still apply: no Monégasque citizens or clergymen are allowed into the gaming rooms.

Casino de Monte-Carlo

Salle des Exhibitions and American restaurant **Stars 'n' Bars**, see page 114.

Return along quai Antoine 1er and from the northeastern corner detour left up to **Église Ste-Dévote** ❽ (daily 8.30am–6pm), dedicated to the principality's patron saint, martyred Corsican virgin Saint Devota, who is said to have drifted ashore here in the 4th century. Although reconstructed in the 19th century and hemmed in by flyovers, the church has a strong symbolic importance for Monégasques, who burn a boat on the parvis every 26 January on the eve of the saint's feast.

Return to the port, following **quai des États-Unis**, where ogling the swanky yachts is a favourite pastime, to the new counter-jetty, part of the port's recent expansion. Now take the footpath that winds round the huge 1970s Les Spélugues complex, a series of overlapping hexagons, containing hotel, apartments and the Auditorium Rainier III congress centre, which juts out on concrete stilts into the water.

MONTE-CARLO

You emerge on avenue Princesse Grace, where the pretty **Jardin Japonais** ❾ (daily 9am–sunset; free) provides an oasis of oriental calm, with streams traversed by stepping stones and wooden bridges, Shinto shrines, raked gravel and trees trimmed into sculptural forms. Behind it is the polygonal glass and copper **Grimaldi Forum** ❿ (www.

grimaldiforum.com), a busy congress, concert and exhibition centre overlooking the sea. It is worth going inside to check out the big summer art show or for a drink or meal at chic bistro **Café Llorca**, see page 113.

Nouveau Musée National de Monaco

Located in exotic gardens across the street, the **Nouveau Musée National de Monaco** ⓫ (www.nmnm.mc; daily June–Sept 11am–7pm, Oct–May 8am–6pm; charge), which is housed in the peaches-and-cream Villa Sauber, could hardly be a greater contrast. This is one of two locations of Monaco's national museum (the other is in Villa Paloma at 56 boulevard du Jardin Exotique, which focuses on art and territory), whose collection is based on the themes of art and performance. Exhibits include a magnificent collection of costumes from the Principality's opera and ballet companies, plans and models of Monaco and temporary art exhibitions.

To the east along avenue Princesse Grace is the **Plage du Larvotto**, Monaco's man-made beach, but to continue this walk take the lift next to the museum up to boulevard des Moulins. Turn left (west) past elegant antiques dealers and clothes shops.

Place du Casino

Just after the **Tourist Office** (see page 129), the manicured fountains and

Jardin Exotique

herbaceous borders of the **Jardins Boulengrin** provide a fine vista down to **place du Casino**, the ensemble that encapsulates the Monte-Carlo myth. To the right, Rolls-Royces and Ferraris line up outside the **Hôtel de Paris**, first and still grandest of Monte-Carlo's grand hotels. On the corner, Cartier heralds the jewellers and couture boutiques that lead up avenue des Beaux-Arts to the palatial Hôtel Hermitage.

On the opposite side of the place du Casino, the terrace of the **Café de Paris**, see ❸, is perfect for observing the comings and goings on the square; within, its slot machines are busy from early morning and a notice at the entrance to the brasserie tells you to check your fur coat into the cloakroom.

For a cheaper pit stop, take avenue des Spélugues for **Le Tip Top**, see page 114, where photos of important customers hang behind the bar.

Finish your walk at the legendary **Casino de Monte-Carlo** ⓬ (www.casino montecarlo.com; daily 2pm–late; over 18s only, ID required). Even if you are not a gambler, the ornate confection still has an aura of glamour. Inside, roulette and black jack are played against a backdrop of allegorical paintings and chandeliers, and across the foyer the **Salle Garnier** opera house, designed by Charles Garnier, has been painstakingly restored right down to the five different shades of gold leaf. Guided tours are available (charge) from 9am to 12.30pm.

Food and Drink

❶ CASTELROC

Place du Palais; tel: +377-93 30 36 68; www. castelroc.com; Mon and Sun L only, Tue–Sat L and D; €€
This institution, with a cheerful, frescoed dining room and elegant conservatory overlooking the palace, is the place to try Monaco's Italianate specialities, such as *stocafi* (stockfish).

❷ LA RASCASSE

1 quai Antoine 1er; tel: +377-93 25 56 90; www.larascassemontecarlo.com; daily D only; €€

A two-storey club that serves 'finger food' such as Tex Mex chicken and hosts live rock bands at night, with a grandstand view of the famous Rascasse bend.

❸ CAFÉ DE PARIS

Place du Casino; tel: +377-98 06 76 23; www.casinocafedeparis.com; daily L and D; €€€
A faithful recreation of the original Belle Époque bar and brasserie, next to the casino. There's great people-watching on the pavement terrace, plus a restaurant with 1900s decor and its own casino with car-themed slot machines. The *crêpe suzette* was invented here. Serves all day.

MENTON

Famed for its mild climate and exotic vegetation, the most Italian of the French Riviera towns is worth exploring for its labyrinthine Old Town, lush tropical gardens and vestiges of its past as an aristocratic winter resort.

DISTANCE: 3.25km (2 miles)
TIME: A full day
START: Jardin Biovès
END: Jardin Botanique Exotique Val Rahmeh
POINTS TO NOTE: Begin in the morning when the market is in full swing. The Jardin Biovès is easily reached from Menton train station along avenue de la Gare. From the Jardin Botanique Exotique Val Rahmeh return to the town centre along the seafront.

Set against a backdrop of mountains just before the Italian frontier, Menton became established in the 13th century on a rocky promontory on the old Roman road from Italy. From 1346, it was ruled by the Grimaldis of Monaco until 1848 when the town declared independence in protest against high taxes on lemons and olive oil, and then voted to become part of France in 1860. Soon it became a favourite destination of the British, Germans and Russians, thanks to Dr Henry Bennett who prescribed the health ben-

efits of winters by the sea. Belle Époque villas, grand hotels, Anglican and Russian Orthodox churches were built and green-fingered visitors, many of them English, made the most of the exceptional climate (Menton claims to have 316 sunny days a year) to introduce tropical plants.

MODERN MENTON

Jardin Biovès

Start your walk down the palm- and orange-tree lined **Jardin Biovès ❶**. Laid out as an elegant promenade over the River Cenci at the end of the 19th century, for two weeks each February it becomes the focus of Menton's Fête du Citron (see page 23), when its lawns are filled with giant sculptures made out of oranges and lemons. The distinctive oval-shaped lemon is noted for its gorgeous scent and unacidic flavour. About halfway down, on avenue Boyer, the fanciful **Palais de l'Europe ❷**, once the grand casino, is now home to the **Tourist Office** (see page 129), municipal library and a contemporary art gallery.

Idyllic Menton

The **Casino** ❸, fronting the sea at the southern end of the gardens, was built in the 1930s with a wavelike Art Deco silhouette. As if in disapproval, the Anglican Church of St John's, an incongruous Victorian Gothic building, turns its back on the casino, although the gambling there is quietly genteel compared to the glamour of nearby Monaco.

Promenade du Soleil

Go round to the right of the casino to the **promenade du Soleil**, which borders the long pebble beach and is lined with an eclectic mix of Belle Époque villas, modern apartment blocks and hotels, and brasseries that do a hard sell with their pavement terraces (try **Restaurant-** **Pizzeria des Artistes**, see ❶, near the casino).

Follow the promenade eastwards, then turn left up rue Adhémar de Lantagnac, turning right at the roundabout into avenue Félix Faure then left into rue Max Barel and first left into rue de la République. Here, you might want to pause for a drink or meal at **Le 5** in Hôtel Mediterranée, see page 114.

Salle des Mariages

From the restaurant, cross the small garden square to the Hôtel de Ville to visit the **Salle des Mariages** ❹ (tel: 04 92 10 50 00; Mon–Fri 8.30am– 12.30pm, 2–5pm; charge), which was decorated by the artist, poet and film-maker Jean Cocteau in the 1950s. Ring

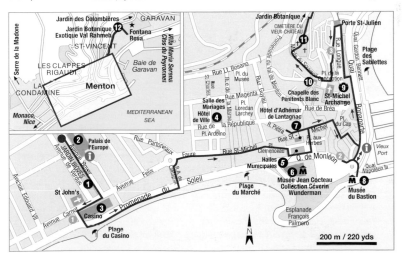

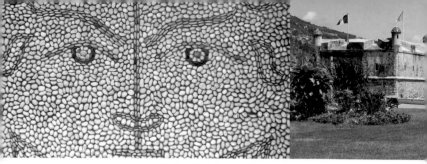

Bastion Musée Jean Cocteau mosaic

ahead to check, as it is sometimes booked up by tour groups and is still used for ceremonies.

After the town hall's classical exterior, the room comes as a vibrant, jazzy surprise from the whimsical murals to the Spanish chairs, mock panther carpet and lamps shaped like prickly pears. For the murals, Cocteau's aim was to 'create a theatrical setting... to offset the officialdom of a civil ceremony', and his inspiration was the Riviera style at the turn of the 20th century, 'a mood redolent of Art Nouveau villas decorated with swirling seaweed, irises and flowing hair'. On the wall above the official's desk, Cocteau depicts the engaged couple – she wears a Mentonnais straw hat, he's in a fisherman's cap – trying to read the future in each other's eyes.

Halles Municipales

Return to avenue Félix Faure, which soon runs into the busy pedestrianised rue St-Michel. On the right at the end of place Clémenceau is the **Halles Municipales** ❺, a covered market, adorned with a glazed ceramic frieze of comical sculpted faces, which offers a profusion of local produce every morning. Look out for Menton lemons, award-winning bakery Au Baiser du Mitron and the socca stalls along the north outside wall for a quick and cheap snack. A short walk to the east in place Docteur Fornari is Les Saveurs d'Eléonore, which stocks a variety of artisanal Menton specialities.

Musée Jean Cocteau – Collection Séverin Wunderman

Opposite the Halles Municipales on the seafront is the new shining star in Menton's cultural galaxy: the **Musée Jean Cocteau Collection Séverin Wunderman** ❻ (2 quai de Monléon; www.musee cocteaumenton.fr; Wed–Mon 10am–6pm; charge). Designed by Bandol-based architect Rudy Ricciotti, who was also one of the architects responsible for the new Department of Islamic Art at The Louvre in Paris, the striking museum opened in 2011. It houses works from the archive of Belgian collector Séverin Wunderman, which he donated to the city in the years leading up to his death. The permanent exhibition changes annually and looks at a different theme of the artist/poet/filmmaker's work.

Rue St-Michel

From here, head up place aux Herbes back to Rue St-Michel. Along with a lot of tourist tack, you can sample real Menton lemon juice and beer (near the junction with rue Pièta) brewed in the nearby village of Castillon at **Mare Nostrum**, and take your pick from dozens of lemon-based products at Au Pays du Citron (no. 24). Next door, the elegant **Hôtel d'Adhémar de Lantagnac** ❼ (tel: 04 92 10 97 10; Tue–Sat 10am–12.30pm, 1.30–6pm), belonging to the Service du Patrimoine, has exhibitions on Menton's architectural heritage.

Now cross place du Cap, just to the east, where **L'Ulivo**, see page 115, and

The 17th-century bastion   *Menton is famous for its lemons*

other restaurant terraces cluster around an olive tree, and descend tiny rue Capierra and rue du Jonquiers to the seafront.

Musée du Bastion Cross the street to the **Vieux Port**, where the 17th-century bastion on the western jetty houses the **Musée du Bastion** ❽ (tel: 04 93 57 72 30; Wed–Mon 10am–noon, 2–6pm; charge). The tiny museum, created by Jean Cocteau, is quickly viewed but has the charm of a scenography overseen by the artist himself, although he died shortly before it opened in 1966. Cocteau adapted his graphic style to the pebble mosaics or *calades* characteristic of the town – a young couple and a schematised face gaze out from either side of the entrance and *La Salamandre* covers the floor downstairs. In the upstairs guards' room, still with its brick oven, changing displays of drawings, lithographs and archive photos focus on Cocteau's Mediterranean period, along with engaging pottery jars influenced by Greek and Etruscan designs.

Across the street from the Musée du Bastion, **Le Nautic**, see ❷, is another possible lunch spot.

VIEUX MENTON

Now follow **quai Bonaparte** north. Amid pavement restaurants, go through a discreet colonnade to the Rampes St-Michel, a steep double flight of steps with pebble *calades* climbing up to the church. Halfway up, turn left then right onto **rue Longue**. This was once Menton's main thoroughfare; Prince Honoré II of Monaco had a palace here in the early 17th century. The street still feels like an Italian hill village, with its tall orange houses, some of them still occupied by craftsmen, and countless dark stairways and alleys leading off on either side.

Consider stopping at no. 66, where **A Braïjade Méridiounale**, see ❸, is an atmospheric place for trying Mentonnais specialities.

Basilique St-Michel Archange

At **Porte St-Julien**, one of the original town gateways, double back along rue Mattoni until a fanciful archway brings you out at the **Basilique St-Michel Archange** ❾ (Mon–Fri 10am–noon and 3–5pm, Sat–Sun 3–5pm; free), a highlight of the region's Baroque architecture. Its campanile dominates Menton's skyline, and the square in front, paved with a grey-and-white pebble *calade* of the Grimaldi coat of arms, is the setting for Menton's prestigious chamber music festival each August (see page 22). The church was begun in 1640, although its sculpted pink-and-ochre façade was rebuilt in 1819. The interior, restored after the 1887 earthquake, is surprisingly large with an arcaded triple nave, crystal chandeliers, elaborate side chapels, and a flamboyantly painted ceiling depicting St Michael slaying the dragon.

Chapelle des Pénitents Blancs

In the adjacent square stands the ornate **Chapelle des Pénitents Blancs** ❿, or

Chapelle de l'Immaculée Conception, which was built in 1687 for a lay confraternity who sought to return to a simpler faith. If you are lucky enough to be here on a Wednesday afternoon (3–5pm if volunteers are present; free) or during the music festival, when it is used for early evening concerts by up-and-coming young musicians, you can visit the beautifully restored interior. Almost life-size stone statues of saints in niches ring the walls and a Baroque ceiling represents Heaven as a Mediterranean paradise. The chapel looks particularly astonishing during certain religious festivals when the walls around the statues, columns and pulpit are entirely covered in red satin hangings.

Cimetière du Vieux-Château

Go round the right-hand side of the chapel and take the steep montée du Souvenir. A gateway on the right leads into the **Cimetière du Vieux-Château** ⓫ (May–Sept daily 7am–8pm, Oct–Apr daily 7am–6pm; free), built on the site of the medieval castle, which was demolished in 1807 after being appropriated as state property following the French Revolution. The slightly dilapidated lower tiers mainly contain British, German and Russian tombs, crowded with memorials to retired surgeons and major generals and the wives and daughters of good families. Overlooking the sea, the grave of the Reverend William Webb Ellis is full of tributes to the man 'who with a fine disregard for the rules of football first took the ball in his arms and ran with it, thus originating the distinctive feature of the rugby game'. A little further along is an elaborate Russian chapel complete with onion dome and coloured tiles, which commemorates a Russian prince.

GARAVAN

Leave the cemetery to the north on place du Cimetière, where a viewing terrace

---

Tropical Gardens

East of Val Rahmeh are four more remarkable gardens, which can be visited by appointment with the Maison du Patrimoine (tel: 04 92 10 33 66): poetic Jardin des Colombières (created in 1919–27) was inspired by Greek and Roman mythology, mixing Mediterranean vegetation and antique sculpture; Fontana Rosa (dating from the 1920s) features tiled pergolas and pools; palm-filled gardens at Villa Maria Serena (built in the 1880s and designed by Charles Garnier); and the Clos du Peyronnet, created by the Waterfield family in 1915, around steps of water.

On the other side of town, the romantic gardens of the Serre de la Madone (74 route de Gorbio; tel: 04 93 57 73 90; Tue–Sun 10am–5pm, summer until 6pm; charge) were designed in the 1920s by Lawrence Johnston, creator of the garden at Hidcote Manor in England, with geometric pools, terraces and rare flora from around the globe.

Blooms from the Jardin Botanique Exotique Val Rahmeh

brings you out onto **boulevard de Garavan**, laid out in 1883 when the prosperous suburb of Garavan was being built with lavish villas and luxuriant gardens. The roadside is draped with bougainvillea, mimosa, succulents, cypresses and other exotic trees, some of which are labelled at pavement level.

Jardin Botanique Exotique Val Rahmeh

Several footpaths lead down to the Garavan seafront. After 36bis Villa Aurélia, take the unkempt sentier de la Villa Noël down between terraced gardens to the **Jardin Botanique Exotique Val Rahmeh** ⑫ (tel: 04 93 35 86 72; Wed–Mon May–Aug 10am–12.30pm and 3.30–6.30pm, Sept–Apr 10am–12.30pm and 2–5pm; guided visits on Monday pm via the tourist office; charge); turn left on avenue St-Jacques for the entrance.

This fascinating botanical garden, now run by the Muséum National d'Histoire Naturel in Paris, was created in the 1920s by retired governor of Malta, Lord Percy Radcliffe, around a villa and lily pond. In the 1950s, the next owner introduced numerous plants from Asia, Africa and the Americas, notably the pretty but poisonous daturas that earned her the nickname 'La Dame aux Daturas'.

A winding trail leads round between magical and medicinal plants, dry and wet environments, towering palms, dank tropical ferns, forests of bamboo and exotic cocoa, avocado, banana, guava and citrus fruits, tea bushes and spice trees, and even the mythic Sophoro Toromiro tree, which is now extinct on its native Easter Island.

Food and Drink

① RESTAURANT-PIZZERIA DES ARTISTES
1080 Promenade du Soleil; tel: 04 93 35 58 50; Mon D, Tue–Sun L and D; €€
Popular with locals and tourists alike. The tables outside on the seafront promenade are the real draw here, but it also serves up competent brasserie fare, such as king prawns, mussels, duck fillet and summer salads.

② LE NAUTIC
27 quai de Monléon; tel: 04 93 35 78 74; daily L and D; €€
A good fish restaurant with friendly Italian owners, located opposite the Musée du Bastion. Try generous portions of fried squid, John Dory with courgettes or sea bass cooked in a salt crust, and the strawberry sabayon for dessert.

③ A BRAÏJADE MÉRIDIOUNALE
66 rue Longue; tel: 04 93 35 65 65; www.abraijade.com; L Sun–Fri, D daily; €€
Authentic regional cooking is served in an ancient beamed dining room hidden in the Old Town. Specialities include vegetable fritters, flame-grilled skewered meats and fish, *ravioles au pistou*, and *bagna caouda* or *anchoïade*.

VENCE

Still ringed by ramparts and a curving wall of buildings punctuated by gateways, the historic centre of Vence forms an attractive labyrinth, where traces of the Roman town of Ventium can still be seen amid the medieval lanes.

DISTANCE: 1km (0.75 mile)
TIME: A half day
START: Place du Grand Jardin
END: Château de Villeneuve – Fondation Emile Hugues
POINTS TO NOTE: From Nice get to Vence via Cagnes-sur-Mer (either taking the M6007 or the autoroute E80) then take the M336 and park in the car park under Place du Grand-Jardin; you can also take a bus (nos 400 or 94) from Nice via Cagnes-sur-Mer or a taxi from Cagnes-sur-Mer.

Vence has a chequered history. It was occupied by the Phoenicians and the Gauls. The Romans named it Ventium and made it an important religious centre when the town converted to Christianity early on, a change usually attributed to St Trophime. The first bishopric was founded here in AD 374, and the town quickly became an important regional centre. The Lombards ravaged the region at the fall of the Roman Empire, and they were followed by the equally destructive Saracens.

Old Vence's two main sights – the old cathedral and former château of the lords of Villeneuve – point to the power struggle between bishops and nobility that long dominated the town. With the eruption of the French Revolution in 1789, Bishop Pisani was forced to flee the country and the see was never restored. Vence drifted into a steady decline so that by the beginning of the 20th century, it was half deserted, with many houses in ruins. After World War I, writers and artists including André Gide, D.H. Lawrence (who died here in 1930), Raoul Dufy, Marc Chagall and Chaim Soutine were drawn to the town. Today, tourism and sunbelt industries have transformed Vence into a bustling centre of more than 17,000 people.

Start your walk at **place du Grand-Jardin ❶**, situated on the edge of the historic centre and home to the **farmers' market** (Tue–Sun am), a **flea market** on Wednesdays, Les Nuits du Sud summer world music festival (see page 22), the **Tourist Office** (see page 130), and several bistros and cafés, including **La Régence**, see ❶.

Vence's well-preserved walled and oval Old Town defies the urban sprawl

PORTE DU PEYRA

From the northeastern corner of the square, cross avenue Henri Isnard and go through the **Porte du Peyra** ❷, an arched gateway through the city wall, adjoining a fortified 12th-century tower. The ramparts were built in the 13th and 14th centuries and once had a broad walk running along the top. A tablet proclaims the virtues of the **Source de la Foux**, a spring bringing delicious fresh calcium-rich water from the mountain to the drinking fountain beneath and the adjacent 19th-century urn-shaped fountain. Behind on the **place du Peyra**, probable forum of the Roman city of Ventium, ancient chestnut trees shade the café and restaurant terraces, and the **Poterie du Peyra** provides a tasteful selection of Provençal pottery, table

linen and kitchenwares. The medieval centre of Vence is very picturesque and, once you get away from the souvenir sellers, the lanes and alleyways are little changed from previous centuries.

Cross the square and turn right into narrow **rue du Marché**, where the former ground-floor stables and kitchens now contain excellent food shops, including **Poivre d'Âne**. Turn left up ruelle de la Mairie to place Clémenceau, home to the **Hôtel de Ville** (town hall), inaugurated in 1911 on the site of the former bishop's palace. Here you will also find some good restaurants including **Les Agapes** ❶.

CATHÉDRALE

To its right is the **Cathédrale** ❸, built between the 12th and 15th centuries on the site of an earlier Merovingian church which was in turn built on top of a Roman temple dedicated to Mars. From 374 until the French Revolution, Vence was a bishopric and had a tradition of powerful clerics: the bishops Véran (5th century) and Lambert (12th century) were both declared saints, while Farnese (16th century) declined the Vence bishop's crosier, going instead to the Holy See to become Pope Paul III. He proved to be quite generous to Vence, how-

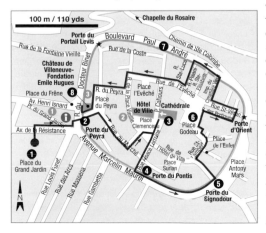

The distinctive white-and-blue Chapelle du Rosaire

ever, and donated several reliquaries.

The unusual side entrance has painted cherubs over the doorway and Roman tablets inserted into the pilasters on either side of the door.

Inside is a triple-naved Romanesque structure with numerous fragments of Carolingian carving from the earlier church incorporated into the walls and columns. Set into an elaborate sculpted frame behind the font is a delicate mosaic designed by Chagall, depicting

Matisse's Chapel

On the outskirts of Vence towards St-Jeannet, the Chapelle du Rosaire (468 avenue Henri Matisse; tel: 04 93 58 03 26; Mon, Wed and Sat 2–5.30pm, Tue and Thur 10–11.30am and 2–5.30pm; charge) is the spiritual masterpiece of Henri Matisse (1869–1954). It was designed between 1947–51 in gratitude to the young Dominican nun Sister Jacques-Marie, who had nursed and sat for him when he was living in Vence during World War II. The elderly artist conceived everything from the building itself, with its blue-and-white glazed pantiles and simple lancet windows, to the gilded crucifix on the altar. The calm interior is a wonderful mix of Matisse's mastery of line, as seen in *St Dominic, the Virgin and Child* and the *Stations of the Cross* drawn in black on white tiles, and of colourful stained glass, the reflections of which send dapples of yellow and green across the walls.

the baby Moses in his cradle in the bulrushes against a sparkling sun. Also worth admiring are the 15th-century oak and pearwood choir stalls carved by Jacques Bellot of Grasse, alive with animals, plants and sometimes irreverent details of clerical life.

ALONG THE MOAT

Leave the cathedral and double back across the square into rue Alsace Lorraine to take the **Porte du Pontis ❹**, which is a vaulted passage that emerges onto avenue Marcelin Maurel. This was once the moat that divided the walled town from the outer *faubourgs* (districts).

Turn left and follow what is now a busy shopping street until place Antony Mars, and return to the old city through the 13th-century **Porte du Signadour ❺** into rue de l'Hôtel de Ville.

Turn right down **rue St-Lambert**, a characterful medieval street, taking a look on the way at the archway, on the right with a Roman stele inserted into the wall, which leads into evocatively named place de l'Enfer (Hell).

AROUND PLACE GODEAU

At the end of rue St-Lambert, turn left into **place Godeau ❻**, the pleasant tree-lined square behind the cathedral, named after 17th-century poet bishop Antoine Godeau, who was a founder member of the Académie Française. In the centre is a granite Roman column.

To the right of the narrow Gothic doorway at no. 5, take rue des Portiques, which overlies part of the Roman road between Cimiez and Castellane, and turn left at the end into rue St-Véran, one of the main thoroughfares through the town. Explore the series of narrow, stepped streets such as impasse du Cimetière Vieux, rue Ste-Élisabeth, rue Pisani and rue Ste-Luce, which lead off it to **boulevard Paul André ➐**, where the once imposing ramparts have been cut down to provide beautiful views of Les Baous mountains.

CHÂTEAU DE VILLENEUVE

Take rue Pisani into **rue de l'Evêché**, full of craft galleries and artists' studios.

Head west back to place du Peyra. On the edge of the square is the rear entrance of the **Auberge des Seigneurs**, see ➌, a historic inn that is still a fine place to stay or eat. Also here is the **Château de Villeneuve – Fondation Emile Hugues ➑** (tel: 04 93 58 15 78; Tue–Sun 10am–12.30pm and 2–6pm; charge), the 17th-century mansion of the lords of Villeneuve, which can be entered through the bookshop beside Porte du Peyra or from place du Frêne.

Inside, leading off a grandiose balustraded staircase, are well-restored, light-filled rooms as well as a tiny square *cabinet* (tiny room) with a frescoed ceiling, which are used for interesting temporary exhibitions of modern and contemporary art.

Leave the Château on place du Frêne, where the ash tree in the centre is supposed to have been planted in 1538 in honour of the visit by François 1er and Pope Paul III.

Fortified Antibes

ANTIBES

Historic Antibes is a year-round destination with its busy yacht harbour, one of the best food markets on the Riviera, and a fascinating collection of works by Picasso in the beautifully restored castle.

> **DISTANCE:** 2.25km (1.5 miles)
> **TIME:** A half day
> **START/END:** Port Vauban
> **POINTS TO NOTE:** If arriving by car, park along the port and avoid driving in Vieil Antibes itself, which is semi-pedestrianised and has a complicated one-way system.

Layers of history are piled up in fortified old Antibes as its medieval buildings sit above those of its Ancient Greek and Roman predecessors. The town began life as the Greek city of Antipolis, "the town opposite," facing Nice. The Greeks held only a narrow stretch between the sea and the present cours Masséna; it was a narrow enclosure filled with warehouses and only one gate, entered opposite the present **Hôtel de Ville** on the cours Masséna at the rue Pardisse. The settlement traded with the Ligurian tribes but did not allow them to enter the city so all dealing took place outside the city walls. The Romans later built an important city here.

Antibes was a keystone in French naval strategy against the Comté of Nice, facing it across the Baie des Anges, and powerful Genoa further east. Sacked twice by Emperor Charles V in the 16th century, Kings Henri II and Henri III added new fortifications, including the Fort Carré.

In 1680, Louis XIV brought in his brilliant military engineer Vauban to give the town the impressive set of star-shaped ramparts and bastions that line the shore, using stone from the ruins of the Roman town, which withstood sieges in 1707 and 1746.

Unlike the holiday hedonism of adjacent Juan-les-Pins (a favourite with F. Scott Fitzgerland and where the concept of summer holidays began) and the exclusive Cap d'Antibes, Antibes itself has a lived-in, all-year appeal with its cobbled shopping streets, lively cafés and a big expat community serving the yachting fraternity.

PORT VAUBAN

Now the largest yacht marina in Europe with berths for over 2,000

Plage de la Gravette

boats (including some of the world's largest and most expensive yachts which line the east quay), spawning a whole industry of shipbrokers, outfitters and crews, **Port Vauban ❶** gave Antibes its strategic importance, especially when Antibes was a stronghold of the French crown against Genoese-ruled Nice. On the southeastern corner of the Vieux Port, a small archway leads through the harbour wall to the **Plage de la Gravette**, a small sandy beach.

Porte Marine

Go through the **Porte Marine ❷**, long the sole entrance to the town from the port, through La Courtine defensive wall, which still has cannon barrels sticking out to sea, into rue Aubernon. On your left, the rampe des Saleurs, recalling the fish salting activity that used to take place here, brings you out to the rampart walk along promenade Amiral de Grasse; note the plaque on the house where painter Nicolas de Staël lived in 1954–5.

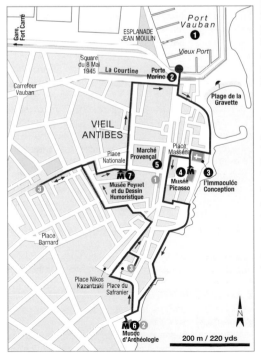

VIEIL ANTIBES

A little further on, go through the arch on rue des Arceaux to enter the pretty maze of small streets and houses of Vieil Antibes. Turn left down rue St-Esprit to the forecourt of the **Église de l'Immaculée Conception ❸**. Its ochre and russet classical façade hides a much earlier structure, which even had the status of cathedral from the 5th century until 1236. The interior is surprisingly simple with no side chapels but plenty

Musée Picasso

of gaudy gilded side altars and a Romanesque east end. The square Romanesque bell tower in front is a converted 12th-century 'Saracen' watchtower.

Cap d'Antibes

Jutting into the sea between Antibes and Juan-les-Pins, wooded Cap d'Antibes is a millionaire's paradise, home to the famous Hôtel du Cap and the palatial villas of Arab princes and Russian oligarchs. At its summit, the Phare de la Garoupe lighthouse is a pleasant walk from Port de Salis up the stony chemin du Calvaire to the Plateau de la Garoupe, where the Chapelle de la Garoupe (daily 10am–noon and 2.30–5pm) has been a site of pilgrimage for centuries.

Be warned that the nearest you are likely to get to its luxury residences is their imposing gateways. One exception is Villa Eilenroc (460 avenue L D Beaumont; tel: 04 93 67 74 33; Wed 2–5pm, first and third Sat of the month 2–5pm; charge), which was designed by Charles Garnier. You can reach it via the Sentier Tir-Poil coastal footpath, which winds round tiny bays and rocky promontories from Plage de la Garoupe (allow about an hour). The villa's gardens provide the stage for the Musiques au Coeur festival in July. An alternative is a cruise in the Visio Bulle (www.visiobulle.com), which allows you to spy on fish through its glass hull and the reclusive residents of Millionaires' Bay from the deck.

Musée Picasso

On leaving, take the steps to the side of the square up to the severe stone Château Grimaldi, now home to the **Musée Picasso ❹** (tel: 04 92 90 54 20; mid-June–mid-Sept Tue–Sun 10am–6pm (July and Aug Wed and Fri until 8pm), mid-Sept–mid-June Tue–Sun 10am–noon and 2–6pm; charge). Built on the site of the Greek acropolis and Roman *castrum*, the castle was the bishop's palace before becoming a residence of the Grimaldi family from 1385 until 1608, when it and the port were sold to the French crown. It then successively served as residence of the king's governor, town hall, barracks, and then the city's first archaeological museum. Many of the Romanesque features remain, including arched windows and the square tower which dominates the old town, though the building was reconstructed in the 16th century. Some of the tiny inner doorways have very attractive carvings. In 1946, curator and archaeologist Romuald Dor de la Souchère let Picasso, who was living in Antibes with his new companion Françoise Gilot, use the large room on the second floor as a studio. Between September and November, Picasso worked here frenetically. The light and intense colour of the south were incorporated into his work in a series of drawings and paintings of fish, sea urchins, goats, stars and the seashore. He was captivated by the antiquity of the Mediterranean. He invented a mythological cast of characters to inhabit his work: a faun,

Antique stalls

a bearded centaur (undoubtedly himself) and a beautiful nymph (Françoise Gilot). The fishermen provided another source of inspiration, as they had done before the war in his huge painting *Night Fishing at Antibes*. Some of these are on canvas, and X-rays have revealed that Picasso had raided the storerooms and painted over what he regarded as mediocre 19th-century paintings. It was also here that Picasso painted the *Antipolis Suite*, a series of highly stylised, pared-down nudes, often reclining.

Picasso left behind 23 paintings and 44 drawings, which form the focus of the recently enlarged and renovated museum.

The collection

In the former studio are some of the main works Picasso created here, including his celebrated *Joie de vivre* (The Joy of Life), a cheerful frieze of music-playing animals and dancing goats, a monochrome triptych *Satyre, faune et centaure*, the gutsy *Le gobeur d'oursins* (The Sea Urchin Eater) and a study for his sculpture *The Goat*, as well as engaging animal-shaped pottery jugs. Other rooms include two striking, highly simplified reclining nudes, still lifes with fish and sea urchins, and numerous drawings.

Picasso was not the only artist drawn to Antibes, and the museum visit starts on the ground floor with the gestural abstraction of Hans Hartung (1904–89) and the more minimalist style, often combined with gold leaf, of his companion Anna-Eva Bergman.

On the first floor are powerful works by Russian-born abstract artist Nicolas de Staël (1914–55), including *Le Grand Concert*, left unfinished at his death, and *Nude*, showing his use of thinner paint and return to figurative elements at the end of his life. There are also contemporary works by Tapiès, Picabia and Léger, among others; note that these paintings are not always on view during temporary exhibitions.

Before you leave, go out onto the terrace, where bronzes by Germaine Richier (1902–59) gaze out to sea from the ramparts alongside sculptures by Arman and Miro.

Marché Provençal

Return down the steps and turn left beside the town hall into broad cours Masséna, where the iron-framed covered market is home to the wonderful **Marché Provençal** ❺ (June–Aug daily 6am–1pm, Sept–May Tue–Sun 6am–1pm), a rather upmarket food market full of tempting fruit and vegetables, goat's cheeses, *tapenades* and dried sausages; in summer, there's also an afternoon **craft market** (mid-June–mid-Sept Tue–Sun; mid-Sept–mid-June Fri–Sun; from 3pm).

The square is arcaded on one side, with small cafés and specialist food shops. Investigate the unusual **Absinthe Bar** (which is beneath olive oil specialist Balade en Provence), with its entrance round the corner on rue Sade, see ❶.

At the southern end of the square, take

the small flight of steps through the Portail de l'Orme into rue de l'Orme – the two round towers you can see are a remnant of medieval wall, built over Roman foundations – and head back to the ramparts.

MUSÉE D'ARCHÉOLOGIE

Continue along promenade Amiral de Grasse, with views of Cap d'Antibes, to **Golden Beef** restaurant, see ❷, and the 1698 Bastion St-André, the southern extremity of Vauban's defences, which contains the **Musée d'Archéologie** ❻ (mid-June–mid-Sept Tue–Sun 10am–noon and 2–6pm, mid-Sept–mid-June Tue–Sun 10am–1pm and 2–5pm; charge). Finds from archaeological digs and underwater shipwrecks, displayed in two long barrel-vaulted gunpowder rooms, illustrate the past importance of Antibes; among them are the *Galet d'Antibes* (Antibes Pebble), a large oval stone with curious inscriptions dating from the 5th century BC, pots testifying to trade with Greece and Etruria, amphorae and ancient anchors, Roman stelae, funerary urns and a mosaic from a Roman villa.

QUARTIER DU SAFRANIER

From the museum, follow rue du Haut-Castelet left to place Nikos Kazantzaki, which honours the Greek author of *Zorba the Greek* who wrote many of his plays and novels in Antibes. Here, orange and yellow signs announce that you are entering the **Commune Libre du Safranier**,

an arty, boho district, which proudly proclaimed independence in the 1960s and still elects its own mayor and councillors.

Take rue du Bas-Castelet, lined with picturesque small houses amid a profusion of creepers and window boxes, and turn right into rue des Pêcheurs and rue du Safranier to arrive in place du Safranier, where **La Taverne du Safranier**, see page 116, is popular for lunch.

Return to rue du Bas-Castelet, turning left at the end into rue de la Pompe, where, at no. 2, **Boulangerie Veziano** (Wed–Sun 6am–1pm and 4.30–7.30pm) produces superb *tourtes de blettes* – both sweet and savoury versions. Now follow rue des Bains into rue James Close; the latter is full of interesting restaurants, art galleries and craft and jewellery shops.

PLACE NATIONALE

At rue de la République, Vieil Antibes' main shopping street, turn left for a shellfish feast at **L'Oursin**, see ❸, or right to reach **place Nationale**. The square is thought to be on the site of the Roman forum, busy with café terraces under the plane trees in summer and the Christmas market in winter. The column in the middle was a present to royalist Antibes from Louis XVIII in gratitude for keeping Napoleon out after his escape from Elba.

You may want to pop into the **Musée Peynet et du Dessin Humoristique** ❼ (tel: 04 92 90 54 30; Tue–Sun 10am–noon and 2–6pm; charge). The collection centres on drawings by popular cartoon-

Port Vauban in all its glory

ist Raymond Peynet, best known for his whimsical *Les amoureux de Peynet* (Peynet's Lovers), but also features the work of other caricaturists.

TOWARDS PORT VAUBAN

On the opposite side of the square, take rue Thuret and turn right into boulevard d'Aiguillon, a broad street running along the inside of La Courtine defensive wall, which is packed with restaurants and loud expat pubs, such as **The Hop Store** and **The Colonial Pub**, frequented by Antibes' large British yachting set. Set into the casement wall, the **Galerie des Bains Douches** puts on exhibitions in the former municipal bathhouse. Go past the fountain at the end of the street to return to Porte Marine and the port.

Le Fort Carré

Crowning a promontory north of the port, the Fort Carré (avenue du 11 novembre, tel: 06 14 89 17 45; Tue–Sun 11am– 5.30pm; guided tours every 30 mins; charge) is a masterpiece of military engineering. Begun by Henri II in the 16th century and improved by Vauban in the 17th, it has four pointed bastions around a circular central keep. No longer used by the military, it features in the 1983 James Bond movie *Never Say Never Again* and the rampart walk offers superb views.

Food and Drink

❶ L'ABSINTHE BAR

25 cours Masséna; tel: 04 93 34 93 00; June–Aug daily 9am–midnight, Sept–May Tue–Sat 9am–midnight; €€
Located beneath a shop selling Provençal delicacies is this atmospheric cellar bar – complete with bits of Roman masonry – dedicated to the green fairy or absinthe, the favourite drink of the Impressionists. Dozens of varieties of absinthe and pastis are on offer amid a 'museum' of absinthe fountains, advertising memorabilia and strange hats to try on.

❷ GOLDEN BEEF

1 avenue du Général Maizière; tel: 04 93 34 59 86; www.golden-beef.fr; daily L and D; €€€
This fashionable steak restaurant and cocktail bar set into the ramparts has tables inside with views of the open kitchen and outside with views of the sea. As well as Charolais and Limousin, the menu includes beef from the US and Argentina. There are gourmet burgers too.

❸ L'OURSIN

16 rue de la République; tel: 04 93 34 13 46; www.restaurant-loursin.fr; Tue–Sun L and D; €€€
Big platters of shellfish are the speciality at this long-established fish restaurant, which has a nautically themed interior as well as tables outside on the square.

Mural celebrating French filmmaker Jacques Tati

CANNES

The grand hotels and luxury shops of La Croisette make Cannes a magnet for hedonists and the jet set, but a walk around town also reveals a lively food market and picturesque old quarter.

DISTANCE: 4.5km (2.75 miles)
TIME: Two or three hours
START: Palais des Festivals
END: Vieux Port
POINTS TO NOTE: Park in the car park near Marché Forville or the one under the Palais des Festivals. From the train station, turn right on rue Jean Jaurès and descend rue Jean de Riouffé to the Palais des Festivals. If you do not want to shop or visit the museum, then this is also a good walk to do in the evening, when boulevard de la Croisette is colourfully illuminated and the people-watching is as good as by day.

For a town now inextricably associated with film-festival glamour, Cannes had modest origins as a dependency of the monks of Lérins. It remains a town of intriguing contrasts, where show-off La Croisette contrasts with villagey Le Suquet where locals of all ages play *boules* under the trees in front of the town hall.

PALAIS DES FESTIVALS

Begin at the **Palais des Festivals** ❶, which occupies centre stage on the seafront between the Old Port and La Croisette. Although the 1980s building, nicknamed 'the bunker', is uninspiring, it plays a leading role in the drama of the annual two-week Film Festival. Be sure to re-enact the famous climb up the red-carpeted stairs – a photo opportunity not to be missed – and follow the trail of handprints left by actors and directors in the terracotta esplanade below. Despite its 18 auditoria used for a panoply of music industry, advertising and property fairs, luxury tourism and shopping conventions, rock concerts and gala spectacles, there are plans afoot for an expansion and modernisation. The building also contains the **Croisette Casino** (www.lucienbarriere. com) and the **Tourist Office** (see page 129). Cross the street to spy on the action from **Caffé Roma**, see ❶, before heading eastwards along boulevard de la Croisette.

View from La Croisette

LA CROISETTE

Cannes' palm-tree-lined seafront boulevard is a mix of glitz and grandeur, with ritzy hotels, luxury boutiques and a constant parade of open-topped cars. In summer the long sandy beach is almost entirely taken up by private beach concessions, with restaurants, deckchairs and jetties for parascending and water-skiing; although, there is a small, busy public section between the Majestic jetty and the Palais des Festivals (if you do not want to pay for a private beach, head to the Plage du Midi at La Bocca, west of Port Vieux, or the Plage du Mourré Rouge on the eastern side of town). Even in winter you will see leathery-skinned ladies bronzing in bikinis, at the same time as others promenade in fur coats up above.

Nonstop designer labels and jewellers at the start of La Croisette provide great window-shopping. At no. 10, the first of Cannes' triumvirate of grand palace hotels is the **Majestic**, which opened in 1926; it keeps up to date with trendy DJs at its fashionable beach restaurant. Stretching between no. 17 and rue d'Antibes, the **Gray d'Albion** shopping mall offers evening wear, haute jewellery and kids' designer togs.

Detour up rue du Commandant André, where the quadrangle formed with rue des Frères Pradignac and rue du Dr Monod is a focus for nightlife. Many bars, such as **For You**, see ➋, open only in the evening, but Provençal restaurant **La Mère Besson**, see ➌, is a prized address at lunch as well.

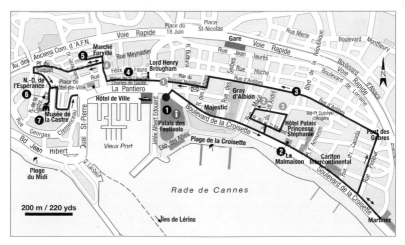

Hôtel Carlton

Grands Hôtels

Back on La Croisette, **La Malmaison ❷** (no. 47; tel: 04 97 06 44 90; July–Aug daily 11am–8pm and until 9pm on Fri, Sept daily 10am–7pm, Oct–Apr Tue–Sun 10am–1pm and 2–6pm; charge) is the former tearoom of the original 19th-century Grand Hôtel, which was replaced by a tower in the 1960s; it is now used for art exhibitions. While the official Film Festival each May is strictly reserved for film industry professionals and the press, there are opportunities to see films during the festival. The Cinéma de la Plage holds free screenings on the beach, while tickets for the Quinzaine des Réalisateurs (www.quinzaine-real-isateurs.com) go on sale at La Malmaison, with screenings in various cinemas around town.

Further along, limos pull up at **Hôtel Palais Princesse Stéphanie**, site of the original Palais des Festivals and still a favourite for festival press conferences.

At no. 58, the **Carlton Intercontinental**, opened in 1912, accommodates the Film Festival jury. The cupolas at either end of its façade were supposedly modelled on the voluptuous breasts of celebrated courtesan La Belle Otero. At no. 73, the Art Deco **Martinez** was France's largest hotel when it opened in 1929 with 476 master bedrooms and 56 bedrooms for clients' personal staff.

AROUND RUE D'ANTIBES

From here La Croisette continues past sun-seeking apartment blocks to Port Canto marina and Pointe de la Croisette. It is more interesting, though, to retrace your steps and take rue Pasteur to **rue d'Antibes ❸**. The street, which follows the former royal carriage route between Toulon and Antibes, is almost entirely dedicated to shopping, mixing mainstream fashion chains with younger, cutting-edge designers. Look up to see fine late 19th-century sculptures, rotundas and wrought-iron decoration, along with remnants of old shopfronts, some of which were once aimed at Cannes' British residents.

The Dawn of Cannes

In 1834, when an outbreak of cholera prevented British Lord Chancellor Henry Brougham from getting to Italy, he back-tracked to the small fishing village of Cannes, where he put up at the simple Hôtel de la Poste (today indicated by a plaque at 4 rue du Port). He liked it so much he stayed, buying a plot of land and building the neoclassical Villa Eléonore on what is now avenue Dr Picard. Cannes' future as an aristocratic winter destination was made. To see some of the villas of the early settlers, explore La Croix des Gardes district west of Le Suquet; the Villa Rothschild (1 avenue Jean de Noailles), set in lovely gardens, is now the municipal library, and Château de la Tour (10 avenue Font-de-Veyre) a comfortable hotel.

Marché Forville

Rue du Bivouac Napoléon
Turn left down rue des Belges and right into **rue du Bivouac Napoléon**, where Napoleon camped out on 1 March 1815, having landed at Golfe-Juan after his escape from exile on Elba. The street today has some relaxed cafés and the **Cannes English Bookshop** at no. 11, a useful source of holiday reading.

ALLÉES DE LA LIBERTÉ

At the end of rue du Bivouac Napoléon, place General Charles de Gaulle opens onto the **Allées de la Liberté ❹**, with its vintage bandstand, *pétanque* pitches and morning **flower market** (Tue–Sun). On the northern side, rue Félix Faure is lined with bars and brasseries, notably seafood institution **Astoux et Brun**, see ❹, and a marble **statue of Lord Henry Brougham** stands on a plinth above a very British-looking lion. On the opposite side is the **Vieux Port** (Old Port), where a few fishing boats sit somewhat incongruously among the luxury yachts.

MARCHÉ FORVILLE

Opposite the pompous 19th-century Hôtel de Ville (Town Hall), take rue Louis Blanc to **Marché Forville ❺** (Tue–Sun 7am 1pm), an animated covered market. In summer it is a feast of tomatoes, aubergines, green figs and piles of garlic, and you can sample *tapenades* and olive oils, although you have to arrive early to find what is left of the local catch.

Running parallel, rue Meynadier is busy with inexpensive clothes and beach gear stores at its eastern end plus some simple restaurants, including **Aux Bons Enfants**, see page 116, nearer the market.

LE SUQUET

At its western end rue Meynadier climbs into rue St-Antoine, start of the picturesque Old Town. Before the arrival of the British in the 19th century, **Le Suquet** was pretty much all there was of Cannes: a few narrow streets and stepped alleyways of tall, yellow and pink houses that still wind up the hill to the fortress constructed by the monks of Lérins. The district is lively at night, when visitors flock to the bars and restaurants on rue St-Antoine and its continuation rue du Suquet.

Notre-Dame de l'Espérance
At place du Suquet turn left up rue Coste-Corail, and then take the traverse de l'Église. This brings you out at the big 17th-century church **Notre-Dame de l'Espérance ❻**, a late example of Provençal Gothic, with a plain, almost unadorned stone façade; the adjoining clock tower is a local landmark. In front, the square is used for concerts in Les Nuits Musicales du Suquet (see page 22). Continue round the side of the church to shady **place de la Castre**, which offers a fine view from its fortified wall.

Eating out in Le Suquet

Musée de la Castre

Entered through a pretty garden at the end of the square, the cool, white-washed rooms of the former castle of the monks of the Iles de Lérins now contain the **Musée de la Castre** ❼ (tel: 04 93 38 55 26; Apr–June and Sept Tue–Sun 10am–1pm and 2–6pm, July–Aug daily 10am–7pm (Wed until 9pm), Oct–Mar Tue–Sun 10am–1pm and 2–5pm; charge). The ethnographic collection, donated by Dutchman Baron Lycklama in 1877, still has the atmosphere of a cabinet of curiosities, with an eclectic array of masks, head-dresses and ceremonial daggers from Tibet, Nepal and Ladakh, bone carvings from Alaska, animal-shaped jugs from Latin America and archaeological finds from Egypt, Cyprus and Mesopotamia. Musical instruments are displayed in the chapel, while three rooms contain paintings by Orientalist and Provençal painters. In the courtyard is the **Tour du Suquet**, an 11th-century watchtower with a panoramic view.

Return to the square; a right turn at the end of rue Perissol will take you into rue Mont Chevalier, which leads back to the Vieux Port. If you wish, you can catch a boat from here to Île St-Honorat to see the monastery where the order of monks who founded the castle live (www.lerins-sainthonorat. com); they are noted for producing good wine and honey.

Food and Drink

❶ CAFFÉ ROMA

1 square Merimée; tel: 04 93 38 05 04; daily L and D; €€
The terrace at this big café is popular day and night for an espresso, cocktails, pasta or simply the ringside view of comings and goings from the Palais des Festivals.

❷ FOR YOU

6 rue des Frères Pradignac; daily 6pm–2.30am
Known for its cocktails and good dance music, this is a fashionable, buzzy place to start a night out. There are regular DJ sets and also a selection of yummy tapas if you fancy a nibble.

❸ LA MÈRE BESSON

13 rue des Frères Pradignac; tel: 04 93 39 59 24; Mon–Sat L and D; €€
Remaining resolutely traditional amid a cluster of trendy lounge bars, the Mother Besson has been serving up Provençal specialities for over half a century.

❹ ASTOUX ET BRUN

27 avenue Félix Faure; tel: 04 93 39 21 87; www.astouxbrun.com; daily L and D; €€
This eternally popular seafood brasserie behind the port is a magnet as much for the superb people-watching as for its big platters of shellfish and it serves food throughout the day. Takeaway dishes are also available.

Grasse, perfume town par excellence

GRASSE

With its challenging topography and the hard sell of the perfumeries on the outskirts of town, Grasse can be a difficult place to grasp. Yet the town merits exploration for its old centre, dynamic perfume museum and the family home of the painter Fragonard.

DISTANCE: 1.5km (1 mile)
TIME: Two or three hours
START: Palais des Congrès
END: Villa Musée Fragonard
POINTS TO NOTE: Grasse has a complicated one-way system, so leave your car in the car park on cours Honoré Cresp. Apart from Fragonard's 'Historic Factory', the main perfume factories (Fragonard, Galimard and Molinard) are located outside the town centre, as are the town's best restaurants.

Grasse grew up around its tanneries before becoming a centre of perfume production. When Catherine de Médicis introduced the Italian fashion for wearing perfumed gloves, the logical step for Grasse's tanneries was to begin producing the necessary scents. By the 18th century, several firms were processing tons of mimosa, needle furze, orange flowers, roses, lavender, jasmine and hyacinths into minute amounts of concentrate for the wealthy. Today, Grasse is one of the most important perfume manufac-

turing cities in the world and, unlike much of the Riviera, it is still essentially a manufacturing town. Grasse's prosperous perfume barons and middle classes hide out in smart bastides in the outskirts, leaving the old centre feeling rather abandoned and surprisingly run down.

Begin on cours Honoré Cresp, which was laid out as a promenade in the 19th century. Here the **Palais des Congrès ❶**, a former casino, is now a congress centre.

MUSÉE INTERNATIONAL DE LA PARFUMERIE

Up the hill, the newly expanded **Musée International de la Parfumerie ❷** (MIP, 2 boulevard du Jeu de Ballon; www.mus eesdegrasse.com; Apr–Sept 10am–7pm, Oct–Mar Wed–Mon 10.30am–5.30pm; charge) displays the assorted plants, minerals, roots and animal matter used for perfumes. A glasshouse contains olfactory plants and materials to sniff and touch. There is also a vast collection of ancient and modern perfume bottles, along with a reconstructed medieval apothecary's shop,

Inside the cathedral

Marie-Antoinette's travelling case, early make-up, and various stills, alambics and equipment. The museum has its own gardens (JMIP; 979 Chemin des Gourettes, Mouans-Sartoux; same website; mid-Mar–mid-Sept daily 10am–7pm, Oct–Nov Tue–Sun 10am–5.30pm; charge), just south of Grasse, which puts an emphasis on biodiversity and traditional methods of cultivation. Visitors can follow an olfactory route, to discover the different flower fragrances, and also visit the conservatory where plants traditionally used to make perfume are grown. There are free guided tours at 5pm from June to August and at 3pm during the rest of the year.

and 19th-century regional costumes and jewellery. A few doors up at no. 14 is the fine doorway of the **Hôtel Luce**, where swashbuckling musketeer d'Artagnan is said to have stayed.

Take a short detour up **impasse des Sœurs**, on the left, to the near derelict-looking medieval house where Queen Catherine de Médicis stayed.

AROUND THE CATHEDRAL

Backtrack to rue Jean Ossola and take rue Gazan to place du Petit Puy. On the left is a square fortified watchtower, and at the rear of the square is the 12th-century **Cathédrale Notre-Dame-du-**

RUE JEAN OSSOLA

Exiting MIP, turn left from boulevard Honoré Cresp into **rue Jean Ossola**, the main thoroughfare of medieval Grasse, lined with *hôtels particuliers*.

On the corner, **Café des Musées**, see ❶, is ideal for a drink or light meal. Across the street at no. 2 is the **Musée Provençal du Costume et du Bijou** ❸ (tel: 04 93 36 44 65; Easter–Oct daily 10am–1pm and 2–6pm, Nov–Easter Mon–Sat; free), an attractively presented private collection of 18th-

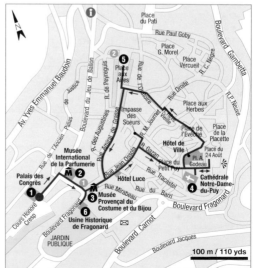

Learn about the perfume process at the Usine Fragonard

Puy ❹ (July–Sept daily 9.30–11.30am and 3–6pm, Oct–June Mon–Sat 9.30–11.30am and 3–5.30pm). The stark west front was altered in the 17th century, when the horseshoe-shaped staircase was added, but the gloomy interior is a heavy example of Provençal Romanesque with huge columns and cursory cross vaulting. To the right of the nave are three canvases by Rubens; in the transept are unusual sculptures of saints and a rare religious painting by Fragonard, *The Washing of the Feet* (1754).

Go through the arch to the left of the cathedral to **place du 24 Août**, a former cemetery with lovely views.

Return through place Godeau and take the steps beside the Hotel de Ville down to **place de l'Evêché**. At the back of the square, a fountain cascades down a row of arches that were originally cellars and warehouses. Cross rue de la Poissonnerie through place Roustan into **rue Rêve Vieille**, which has an eclectic mix of medieval and 18th-century architecture.

PLACE AUX AIRES

Turn left at the end into rue Marcel Journet and right into rue de l'Oratoire, taking rue des Fabreries into the attractive **place aux Aires** ❺. Lined with tall, arcaded, mainly 16th- and 17th-century houses, the square was the original focus of the town's tanning industry. Today there's a small **food and flower market** (Tue–Sun). On a street leading off the western side is **La Voûte**, see ❷.

From the southern end, take rue Amiral de Grasse, home to antiques shops and upmarket clothes shops, which curves back to rue Jean Ossola.

USINE HISTORIQUE DE FRAGONARD

Return to boulevard Fragonard for the **Usine Historique de Fragonard** ❻ (tel: 04 93 36 44 65; daily 9am–6pm; free) at no. 20. Although most of the perfumes are now made at the modern Fabrique des Fleurs outside the centre, the factory founded by Eugène Fuchs in 1926 still makes and packages some perfumes, soaps and cosmetics, and holds a collection of antique stills and perfume bottles.

Food and Drink

❶ CAFÉ DES MUSÉES

1 rue Jean Ossola; tel: 04 92 60 99 00; 8.30am–6.30pm summer daily, winter Mon–Sat; €
This stylish café, set between the perfume and costume museums, serves salads, savoury tarts and home-made desserts.

❷ LA VOÛTE

3 rue de Thouron; tel: 04 93 36 11 43; Mon–Sat L and D; €€
A convivial restaurant where Provençal dishes and meat roasted on an open fire are served in a vaulted room (hence the name) or on a terrace on place aux Aires.

Beach bum

ST-TROPEZ

The legendary Riviera resort of St–Tropez is a bewitching mix of Provençal fishing village and jet–setters' hotspot, with a handful of interesting museums and historical sights.

DISTANCE: 2.25km (1.5 miles)
TIME: Two or three hours
START/END: Vieux Port
POINTS TO NOTE: The biggest problem with St-Tropez is the summer traffic jams. If you do not have your own yacht for swanning into the Vieux Port, use the ferry service from Ste-Maxime with Les Bâteaux Verts (www.bateauxverts.com), which runs several boats an hour in peak season. By car, try to use the back roads from Ramatuelle rather than the road from Ste-Maxime, and avoid aperitif hour and Tuesday and Saturday morning market days. The large car park along the Nouveau Port is just a short stroll from the Vieux Port.

ST-TROP ON SCREEN

Roger Vadim's 1956 film *Et Dieu créa la femme* created both St-Trop's beach image and Brigitte Bardot, while in 1968, Alain Delon, Romy Schneider and a young Jane Birkin lazed around a pool in *La Piscine*. But for many French people

St-Trop on film is inseparably associated with the elastic face of Louis de Funès in the series of cult comedies begun by *Les gendarmes à Saint-Tropez* (1964).

St-Tropez continues to draw the international jet-set, combining, as it does, glamorous resort and authentic Provençal village. For all its showbiz flavour, de-luxe hotels, legendary nightlife, ostentatious yachts and sometimes outright vulgarity of the *m'as-tu vu* (see and be seen) scene, 'St-Trop' still has a surprising charm and even a certain democracy: anyone can dress up and parade along the quays, and those with the right look will be able to make it past the rigorous *physionomistes* (bouncers) of Les Caves du Roy.

VIEUX PORT

From early Roman martyr Torpes, who gave the town its name, via neo-Impressionist Paul Signac to today's party people, visitors have always arrived at St-Tropez by boat. The pretty **Vieux Port** ❶ (Old Port) is still the town's animated heart, lined with tall, colourful houses that were faithfully restored after World

Yachts in the Vieux Port   *Pretty backstreet*

War II damage, and busy quayside bars and brasseries.

Musée de l'Annonciade

Beside the port on place Grammont, the **Musée de l'Annonciade ❷** (tel: 04 94 17 84 10; Wed–Mon 10am–noon and 2–6pm, closed Nov; charge) is one of the region's best museums, with a collection of post-Impressionist and modern art focused on St-Tropez and the Riviera. Among the highlights are pointilliste views of St-Tropez by Signac, Nabis paintings by Vuillard and early Fauve works by Derain, Matisse and Braque.

Maison des Papillons

Cut through to rue Allard, with its boutiques and arcades, and detour up narrow rue Etienne Berny for another

surprising museum, the **Maison des Papillons ❸** (tel: 04 94 97 63 45; Wed, Thu, Sat 10am–12.30pm and 2–6pm, Fri 2–6pm, Sun 10am–12.30pm and 2–5pm; charge), where over 4,000 species of butterfly collected by painter Dany Lartigue are displayed around a small fisherman's house. The painter was the son of famous 1920s society photographer J.H. Lartigue, some of whose photos can be seen in the kitchen.

The quays

Return to the port, where **quai Suffren** is the place in St-Tropez to people watch. Luxury yachts moor sternside to the quay, allowing promenaders to gawp at uniformed flunkeys and on-board cocktail parties, while others try to look nonchalant from the row of portside bars, such

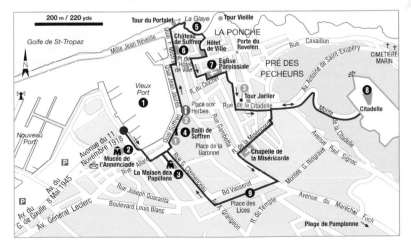

Spice stall at the place des Lices market

as **Bar du Port**, see , and neo-Baroque Café de Paris.

Halfway along, in front of the Hôtel Sube, with its own discreetly fashionable bar on the first floor, is a statue of **Bailli de Suffren** ④ (1729–88), erected in 1866 using bronze from melted-down arms captured from the Royal Navy. One of St-Tropez's most illustrious adopted citizens, Pierre-André de Suffren's nautical career culminated with a successful Indian campaign and the command of the French navy.

Further along, **Le Gorille**, see ②, dispenses drinks and brasserie standards day and night. Opposite, next to the **Tourist Office** (see page 130), a small arch leads to **place aux Herbes**, where there is a small fish market every morning.

A bigger attraction is the red chairs of **Senequier**, see page 118, on **quai Jean Jaurès**, perfect for people-watching at aperitif hour, and the elegant terraces of **Le Quai**, see page 118, and sister fish restaurant, Escale, a few doors up.

On **quai Frédéric Mistral** is a memorial to the navies of France, America and Britain and the Liberation of Provence; Allied forces landed on the Var coast on 15 August 1944.

La Glaye

Walk between the squat round **Tour du Portalet** and restaurant opposite, where the beginning of the coast footpath leads over the rocks to **La Glaye** ⑤, a small cove surrounded by pastel-coloured fishermen's houses.

AROUND THE HÔTEL DE VILLE

From the beach, take the first of the covered archways into rue Sous de la Glaye, which comes out on place de **l'Hôtel de Ville**, where the Hôtel de Ville faces a fine mansion with a carved wooden doorway brought back from Zanzibar in the 1800s by a Tropezian navigator.

At the lower end of the square, the **Château de Suffren** ⑥, though now named after the naval hero, is a remnant of the square tower built by Guillaume, 1st Count of Provence, in 980. It was built to protect the Gulf of St-Tropez's settlements from North African Barbary pirates, whose raids plagued the region until the 15th century.

Take rue Sibille, then turn left up rue de l'Église to **Église Paroissiale** ⑦ (open morning only), St-Tropez's parish church, which contains a carved bust of St Torpes. Take rue du Clocher up the side of the church through place de l'Ormeau and rue de l'Ormeau into rue de la Citadelle, where the triangular rough stone **Tour Jarlier** is a remaining corner of the town ramparts. **Le Dit Vin** ③ is a good place for lunch or dinner.

CITADELLE

At the top of rue de la Citadelle, steps lead across the Pré des Pecheurs to the **Citadelle** ⑧ (www.saint-tropez.fr; Apr–Sept daily 10am–6.30pm, Oct–Mar daily 10am–12.30pm and 1.30–5.30pm; charge), built in the early 17th

Spot the rich and beautiful along quai de Suffren

century for King Henri IV. Although it was the main coastal defence between Antibes and Toulon, the fortress was attacked by Spanish troops in 1637. In 1652 its garrison joined La Fronde rebellion against the king, and the townspeople, with help from Toulon, besieged the castle. The Naval Museum, in the dungeon, was refurbished in 2013; ramparts lined with cannons and the roof terrace of the keep provide fine views.

AROUND PLACE DES LICES

Return to rue de la Citadelle, and at place Forbin turn left along rue du Petit Bal and descend rue de la Miséricorde, marked by the tiled dome of the **Chapelle de la Miséricorde**, into **rue Gambetta**. Here, elegant 18th-century doorways of shipowners' and merchants' houses punctuate upmarket shops, such as **Villebrequin** (nos 24 and 28), homegrown seller of men's swimming trunks.

Continue to **place des Lices **. The big square is where St-Tropez millionaires play at being Provençal villagers, renting *boules* from the **Café des Lices**, see , for a game of *pétanque* under the plane trees and congregating at the chic **food and general market** (Tue–Sat am).

Return to the Vieux Port along **rue Georges Clémenceau**, source of St-Trop's classic strappy centurion sandals from **Atelier Rondini** (no.16) and creamy cakes at **La Tarte Tropézienne** (no.36).

Food and Drink

● BAR DU PORT
7 quai Suffren; tel: 04 94 97 00 54
A sleek, portside vantage point where a designer-clad crowd lounges in white and chrome sofas surveying the passers-by.

● LE GORILLE
1 quai Suffren; 04 94 97 03 93;
www.legorille.com; July and Aug daily 24 hours, Sept–June daily 8am–1am; €
Compared with its hip neighbours, the open-all-hours Gorilla is a refreshingly down-to-earth place serving steak tartare and *salade niçoise* all day, and sustenance for après-clubbers all night long.

● LE DIT VIN
7 rue de la Citadelle; tel: 04 94 97 10 11;
daily L and D; €€
Lively restaurant/tapas bar in a lovely old village house with a roof that opens up in summer. Mediterranean dishes include pasta with truffles and the wine list is reasonable for these parts. Great service too.

● CAFÉ DES LICES
Place des Lices; 04 94 97 44 69;
www.lecafe.fr; daily L and D; €€
A classic café, serving up grilled steaks and Provençal dishes to generations of celebs. Sit on the terrace or in the vintage interior.

MASSIF DES MAURES

A circular driving tour through the wild mountain hinterland of St–Tropez and the scenic Corniche coast road, with footpaths, monasteries, beaches, vineyards and tropical gardens to discover en route.

DISTANCE: About 95km (60 miles)
TIME: A full day
START: Cogolin
END: Domaine de Rayol
POINTS TO NOTE: Distances on this route are not far as the crow flies, but allow plenty of time as some of the mountain roads are hair-raisingly twisty and narrow.

ALL IN A NAME

The Massif des Maures gets its name from *maurus* (the Provençal word for sombre or dark brown), relating to the dark colour of the hills rather than the Moors who occupied them for much of the Middle Ages.

Just minutes from the family resort of Le Lavandou or the bustle of St-Tropez is the thickly forested and surprisingly wild mountains of the Massif des Maures. Timber, chestnut and cork production are still the main activities here, and forestry roads and long-distance footpaths provide great opportunities for hiking.

Cogolin and Grimaud

After the showbiz antics of St-Tropez, **Cogolin** ❶ has the appeal of a real working town, with useful facilities such as a petrol station and supermarket, and home-grown industries (briar pipe and carpet making). Also here is the pretty 11th-century church, Église St-Sauveur St-Étienne, a 14th-century tower and La Demeure Sellier art gallery.

Now take the D558 3.5km (2 miles) north to **Grimaud** ❷, a hill village with a tangle of pretty streets sitting under a set of picturesque castle ruins.

LA GARDE FREINET

Continue northwest for 9km (5.5 miles) through gnarled cork oak woods; look out for trees where the lower section of the trunk has been stripped of its bark for cork production, once the principal activity of **La Garde Freinet** ❸. This small, lively town is home to an attractive main square with a fountain, cafés and a couple of sophisticated homeware shops. It grew up in the 13th century, when the population moved down from

The fortress-like Chartreuse de la Verne

the hilltop settlement that had developed around the Saracen fortress of **Fraxinet**, a steep walk to the northwest.

Return to Grimaud and head west towards Collobrières along the D14.

CHARTREUSE DE LA VERNE

After 20km (12 miles), turn left onto the narrow D214, which climbs up through dense woodland. Leave your car at the car park and continue on foot up to the forbidding, fortress-like Carthu-

sian monastery of the **Chartreuse de la Verne** ❹ (tel: 04 94 48 08 00; Wed–Mon 11am–5pm, June–Aug until 6pm, closed in periods of high fire risk; charge). Founded in 1170 by the Bishop of Toulon, it sits brooding on the hillside in solitary splendour. Apart from the Romanesque church, most of the buildings date from the 17th century and have been rebuilt several times due to fire damage. Abandoned after the Revolution, restoration work began in the 1970s and since 1983 the monastery has been resettled

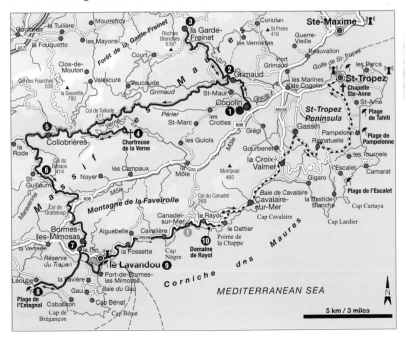

Bormes-les-Mimosas

by a community of nuns. The visit begins in the massive gatehouse, taking in the church, cloister, cemetery, grainstore and a restored monk's cell with a private courtyard for meditation.

COLLOBRIÈRES

Return to the D14, where the road continues along the Réal Collobrier valley to **Collobrières ❺**. The town thrived in the 19th century with the logging industry, and cork oak and chestnut cultivation, when timber barons put up fine houses and the medieval Église de St-Pons was supplanted by a new neo-Gothic edifice. Today, the small, pleasant town is renowned for its sweet chestnuts and has an 11th-century hump-backed bridge, attractive old streets and some simple restaurants, such as the **Hôtel-Restaurant des Maures**, see page 119. Be sure to stop off at Confiserie Azuréenne to sample its chestnut-based sweet treats.

COL DE BABAOU

About 2 km (1 mile) after leaving Collobrières, turn left on the D41 towards Bormes-les-Mimosas. The narrow road winds up endless hairpin bends to the **Col de Babaou ❻** pass at 414m (1,360ft), with fine views of the sea and Iles de Hyères in one direction and the Laquin peak in the other. Some 8km (5 miles) further on at the Col de Gratteloup the road crosses the busy D98. Continue along the D41, which descends into the pretty village of Bormes-les-Mimosas.

BORMES-LES-MIMOSAS

Built strategically on a hill inland from the coast, under the remains of the castle of the Lords of Fos, the village of **Bormes-les-Mimosas ❼** is swathed not just in mimosa, but in colourful bougainvillea and artfully planted agaves and cactuses. Village life centres on the animated place Gambetta, with its cafés and restaurants, such as **La Tonnelle**, see page 119. It leads to the craft and food shops of rue Carnot and other atmospheric streets like rue Ruompi Cuuo.

CAP DE BRÉGANÇON BEACHES

From Bormes descend to the coast by the boulevard du Soleil, turning right through Le Pin. At the roundabout take the D559 towards Le Lavandou. After about 200m/yds, detour right down route de Cabassol towards **Cap de Brégançon** for the best beaches in the area. At the end of the road, turn right (west) passing the cream-coloured wine-producing Château de Brégançon, then turn left to the **Plage de l'Estagnol ❽** (Easter–Oct; parking charge), a beautiful shallow sandy cove with shady pines and the excellent **Resto Plage de l'Estagnol** (tel: 04 94 64 71 11; Apr–Sept daily L and D; reserve for dinner); alternatively, turn left (east) for the **Plage du Cabasson** (parking charge) and the

The Fort de Brégançon, now opened to the public

Fort de Brégançon (www.monuments-nationaux.fr; daily July–Sept 9am–7pm; charge; reservations are obligatory and must be made at the tourist office in Bormes-les-Mimosas), until recently one of the official residences of the French president, but now open to the public.

Return to the D559. At rondpoint (roundabout) de la Baou take the route de Benat and then turn left on avenue de la Mer to Bormes' beach suburb of **La Favière**, which has a long beach of fine golden sand and a marina offering good diving, kayaking and sailing facilities.

LE LAVANDOU

La Favière runs into the family-friendly resort of **Le Lavandou** ❾, where a rather glitzy seafront promenade and long, crowded sandy beach hide a surprisingly pretty little Old Town. At the eastern end of the harbour, the road tunnel brings you back to the D559. A little further on to the right, the curved, steeply shelving beach at St-Clair is the nicest of Le Lavandou's beaches.

DOMAINE DU RAYOL

From here the D559 Corniche des Maures follows the coast eastwards, through Cavalière and up towards the Pointe de la Chappe at Rayol-Canadel, past **Maurin-des-Maures**, see ❶.

Follow signs to the right for the fabulous gardens of the **Domaine du Rayol** ❿ (avenue des Belges, Le Rayol-Canadel; www.domaindurayol.org; daily July–Aug 9.30am–7.30pm, Apr–June and Sept–Oct until 6.30pm, Jan–Mar and Nov–Dec until 5.30pm; charge), created in 1910 by banker Alfred Courmes, who filled the grounds around his house with exotic plants. The Domaine now belongs to the Conservatoire du Littoral coastal trust, which restored the gardens and added species from other Mediterranean-type climates in Australia, southern California, Mexico and Cape Horn. Pick up the leaflet to follow a trail with giant ferns, Australian blackboys and other unusual plants. There is even an underwater *jardin marin* to be visited with snorkel and flippers (guided visit by reservation), as well as classical concerts in summer.

From here you can head to St-Tropez on the D559, or turn right at **La Croix Valmer** (13km/8 miles) to **Gassin** and **Ramatuelle**.

DIRECTORY

Hand-picked hotels and restaurants to suit all budgets and tastes, organised by area, plus select nightlife listings, an alphabetical listing of practical information, a language guide and an overview of the best books and films to give you a flavour of the region.

Eccentric elegance inside the Hôtel Negresco

ACCOMMODATION

Hotels ranging from medieval castles to Belle Époque villas to conceptual modern design buildings are all part of the Riviera experience. Despite a reputation for expensive palaces with sumptuous suites and every imaginable amenity, there are also plenty of affordable places where you will still find a warm welcome, sometimes in lovely settings; just do not expect too much in the way of room service and be prepared to drag your suitcases up the stairs yourself. If you arrive without accommodation, many tourist offices have a last-minute reservation service. Book well ahead for Cannes Film Festival and the Monaco Grand Prix in late May, when hotels are full for miles around and prices can easily double or more. While most hotels in Nice and Cannes are open all year and cater to a congress and business clientele as well as the holiday trade, many hotels in smaller resorts close in winter. Prices indicated in this section are for the peak summer period but prices are often much lower out of season and you can find good internet deals (sometimes even in peak season, especially at the last minute).

Price for a double room for one night in high season, including tax but not breakfast:
€€€€ = over 300 euros
€€€ = 180–300 euros
€€ = 100–180 euros
€ = below 100 euros

Nice

Hi Hôtel
3 avenue des Fleurs; tel: 04 97 07 26 26; www.hi-hotel.net; €€€
A cult address for design buffs, where nine different room concepts encourage you to experiment with new ways of living; try a bath in the middle of the room, a pontoon, four-poster bath and operating table bed… There's an organic snack bar and restaurant and DJs in the bar at weekends. The rooftop sundeck has a minuscule pool and is more suitable for taking a dip than doing lengths.

Hôtel Aria
15 avenue Auber; tel: 04 93 88 30 69; www.aria-nice.fr; €€
Overlooking an attractive garden square amid the Belle Époque and Art Deco buildings of the musicians' quarter, this good-value 19th-century hotel has recently been renovated although it kept the creaky vintage panelled lift. Rooms are light and high-ceilinged and decorated in sunny Mediterranean colours.

Hôtel Beau Rivage
24 rue St-François-de-Paule; tel: 04 92 47 82 82; www.nicebeaurivage.com; €€€
Located near the Opéra, the hotel where Matisse stayed when he first came to

The fabulous chandelier at the Negresco

Nice – as well as Nietzsche and Chekhov – is now a gorgeous exercise in sophisticated minimalism and decorated in natural wood and tones of grey by architect Jean-Michel Wilmotte. Beach pebbles are an underlying theme, from the pebble-shaped pouffes and cushions in Les Galets lounge bar to the pebble lampstands in the 118 rooms and the pebble-floor bathrooms. It also owns the chic Beau Rivage beach, with its huge, teak-decked restaurant.

Hôtel Clair
23 boulevard Carnot; tel: 04 93 89 69 89; www.clair-hotel-nice.com; €
This charming two-star hotel a couple of minutes' walk to the east of the port is arguably the best budget option in town. The 10 individually decorated studios, each opening onto the garden, have kitchenettes and free Wifi. Parking is available at extra cost.

Hôtel Ellington
25 boulevard Debouchage; tel: 04 92 47 79 79; www.ellington-nice.com; €€
This elegant town-centre hotel next to the Théâtre de l'Image et de la Photo was transformed in 2008 as a homage to jazz. Downstairs there is an atmospheric, 1950s speakeasy-style whisky bar, as well as black-and-white photos of jazz musicians in lifts and corridors. Bedrooms vary between black-and-white minimalism and a more traditional Provençal style.

Hôtel Le Grimaldi
15 rue Grimaldi; tel: 04 93 16 00 24; www.le-grimaldi.com; €€
Housed in two Belle Époque buildings, this lovely intimate hotel in the New Town with helpful staff and comfortable good-sized rooms decorated with colourful neo-Provençal fabrics; those on the upper floors have views over the city or Mont Boron.

Hôtel Negresco
37 promenade des Anglais; tel: 04 93 16 64 00; www.hotel-negresco-nice.com; €€€€
Crowned by its pink and green cupola, the Negresco is both Nice's most celebrated hotel and one of its most eccentric, with its mix of elegance and kitsch. Original Old Master paintings and modern sculptures by Niki de St-Phalle mix with gold-plated basins and curiously tacky souvenir shops, and owner Jeanne Augier has personally selected the rooms' antiques and other furnishings. There are two restaurants: the haute-cuisine Chantecler and the merry-go-round themed La Rotonde. There is a private beach in front of the hotel.

Nice Garden Hôtel
11 rue du Congrès; tel: 04 93 87 35 62; www.nicegardenhotel.com; €€
A family-run hotel with nine tastefully decorated rooms, each overlooking the verdant Mediterranean garden – there are even orange trees. Children over the age of six are welcome and it's only 10

minutes' walk from the train station and the beach.

Hôtel du Petit Palais

17 avenue Emile Bieckert; tel: 04 93 62 19 11; www.petitpalaisnice.com; €€
Staying in the intimate ochre-coloured villa in Cimiez that once belonged to actor-playwright Sacha Guitry gives a taste of living in residential Nice. Staff are welcoming and rooms are attractively decorated, some with small terraces or balconies giving views over the rooftops to the Baie des Anges, and there is a small paved garden courtyard. It is near to the Chagall Museum but a bit of a trek to most of the city's restaurants.

Hôtel Suisse

15 quai Raubà Capéù; tel: 04 92 17 39 00; www.hotels-nice-suisse.com; €€€
Behind a period façade and built into the cliff face of Castle Hill, the attractive Hôtel Suisse has been stylishly modernised with a different colour scheme on each floor. Most rooms have a sea view and balcony. The gorgeous, airy ground-floor salon and breakfast room even contains a minuscule rock cave.

Hôtel Villa Les Cygnes

6 avenue Château de la Tour; tel: 04 97 03 23 35; www.villalescygnes.com; €€
Near the Musée des Beaux-Arts on the Baumettes hill, this 1920s three-storey villa now has six elegantly decorated rooms: the two on the ground floor open onto the garden while those on the sec-

ond floor have balconies. There is free Wifi and air-conditioning.

Hôtel Villa Rivoli

10 rue de Rivoli; tel: 04 93 88 80 25; www.villa-rivoli.com; €
This ornate villa, built in 1890 to accommodate winter visitors to the Riviera, has been restored with lashings of charm and 24 tasteful bedrooms, plus staff who strive to make you feel at home. Downstairs, there is a lovely salon in gentle tones of grey and beige, with family portraits, comfortable sofas and bergère chairs around the fireplace, and a small garden. There is air conditioning but no lift.

Hôtel Westminster

27 promenade des Anglais; tel: 04 92 14 86 86; www.westminster-nice.com; €€€
This venerable pink stucco seafront hotel, which opened in 1880, has preserved its impressive ground-floor *salons* and the magnificent open staircase, hung with an interesting collection of historic oil paintings of old Nice. Bedrooms have gradually been redone floor by floor; some in traditional style, the most recent ones in more contemporary soft pearly blues with subtle lighting. There is a restaurant and bar.

Hôtel Windsor

11 rue Dalpozzo; tel: 04 93 88 59 35; www.hotelwindsornice.com; €€
From the outside it looks like any other 19th-century hotel, but within is a true

one-off. Many of the rooms have been individually decorated by internationally renowned contemporary artists; simpler rooms have frescoes or posters. There is a new spa, an outdoor swimming pool and aviary in the lushly planted garden, a restaurant and changing art installations in the hallway.

Villa La Tour

4 rue de la Tour; tel: 04 93 80 08 15; www.villa-la-tour.com; €€

With just 17 rooms located in a former monastery, the Villa La Tour is for romantics who want to stay in the Old Town itself. Squashy decrepit sofas in the entrance and individually decorated rooms have a boho charm. The cheapest rooms overlook a small courtyard; pay slightly more for a view over the Vieux Nice rooftops. No lift.

Villa Victoria

33 boulevard Victor Hugo; tel: 04 93 88 39 60; www.villa-victoria.com; €€

An elegant 19th-century villa with a listed façade in the heart of the New Town. Rooms are rather functional, but are high-ceilinged and of a good size. Some have balconies, but the real treat here is the exotically planted garden, where you can relax in the shade of tall palms and orange trees.

The Corniches

La Bastide aux Camélias

23 route de l'Adret, Èze; tel: 04 93 41 13 68; www.bastideauxcamelias.com; €€

Gorgeous B&B in a renovated 16th-century farmhouse on the outskirts of the village, with amazing views over the coast. The four bedrooms have a romantic air and there's a lovely garden and pool. Book an aromatherapy massage if you need to de-stress.

Château Eza

Rue de la Pise, Èze Villlage; tel: 04 93 41 12 24; www.chateaueza.com; €€€€

Perched high over the Mediterranean, this luxurious 12-room hideaway in a medieval building in the ramparts of Èze has to be one of the most romantic hotels on the Riviera. Bedrooms have pretty *toile de jouy* print fabrics, many have exposed stone walls and stone fireplaces, and some have terraces; the suite even has an outdoor jacuzzi. There is a sleek bar and a gastronomic restaurant with spectacular views. No access to vehicles.

Grand Hôtel du Cap Ferrat

71 boulevard du Général de Gaulle, St-Jean-Cap-Ferrat; tel: 04 93 76 50 50; www.grand-hotel-cap-ferrat.comr; €€€€

Occupying the tip of Cap Ferrat, this Riviera *grande dame* was brought up to date in 2009 in a style that is opulent yet tastefully restrained. Bedrooms in the main building feature bespoke furniture, vast beds and walk-in dressing rooms, while ground-floor suites in the wavelike modern annex each have a private infinity pool. There is also a new spa, although it is hard to beat the beauty of the original

The pool and balconies at the revamped Hôtel du Cap–Ferrat

outdoor infinity pool, reached by a glass-sided funicular. Americans and Russians head the guest list, some of whom stay here for months. The 300 staff will cater to every need and even the tree tops over the restaurant terrace have been manicured like a lawn.

Hôtel Brise Marine

58 avenue Jean Mermoz, St-Jean-Cap-Ferrat; tel: 04 93 76 04 36; www.hotel-brisemarine.com; €€

Expect fairly small but immaculate bedrooms in this authentic late 19th-century villa, which overlooks the Mediterranean. A steeply terraced garden, adorned with palm trees, fountains and flowerpots, leads down to the sea. No restaurant.

La Fiancée du Pirate

8 boulevard de la Corne d'Or, Villefranche-sur-Mer; tel: 04 93 76 67 40; www.fianceedupirate.com; €€

In a residential area above the bay, 'the pirate's girlfriend' has a beach house feel. Some rooms have sea views, some open onto the garden and there are bungalows too. The pool means you don't have to trek to the beach.

Hôtel La Régence – Chez Betty

2 avenue Maréchal Foch, Villefranche-sur-Mer; tel: 04 93 01 70 91; www.laregence-hotel.fr; €

On the main road that runs through Villefranche, above the old town, this café-hotel has 10 rooms which were redecorated in 2013 in modern Provençal style. There

is free Wifi and the bus stop and train station are a stone's throw away. A studio apartment is available nearby.

Hôtel Villa Cap Ferrat

49 avenue Denis Semeria, St-Jean-Cap-Ferrat; tel: 04 93 76 24 24; www.hotel-villa-cap-ferrat.com; €€€

Formerly Hôtel Belle Aurore, this three-star hotel on Cap Ferrat reopened in 2014 after total renovation to turn it into modern, stylish accommodation. Seventeen rooms overlook the bay and the 20 metre pool, where the breakfast buffet is served.

Hôtel Welcome

3 quai Amiral Courbet, Villefranche-sur-Mer; tel: 04 93 76 27 62; www.welcome hotel.com; €€€

With the best location in Villefranche, right on the quayside next to the Cocteau Chapel, it is not surprising that this historic hotel has welcomed all sorts of illustrious guests over the past 200 years. The spacious airconditioned rooms nearly all have balconies overlooking the port, and the former restaurant has been replaced by a stylish yet relaxed wine bar. Closed mid-November–Christmas.

Monaco

Hôtel Columbus

23 avenue des Papalins; tel: +377 92 05 90 00; www.columbushotels.com; €€€

In Fontvieille, this was Monaco's first boutique hotel and a favourite with rac-

Breathtaking sea view at the Hôtel du Cap–Ferrat

ing drivers as it was once owned by David Coulthard. Accommodation is in stylish rooms, suites and an apartment. There's a sleek restaurant serving Asian-Fusion cuisine and an outdoor pool.

Hôtel Miramar

1 avenue Président J.-F. Kennedy, La Condamine; tel: +377-93 30 86 48; www.miramarmonaco.com; €€€

A bargain 11-room hotel above a modern brasserie with fine views across the Port Hercule to the Palais Princier on the other side. Rooms are bright and stylish with a vaguely nautical theme; some have balconies. Staff are friendly.

Hôtel de Paris

Place du Casino, Monte-Carlo; tel: +377-92 16 30 00; www.hoteldeparismontecarlo. com; €€€€

As much a part of Monte-Carlo's history as the Casino at the end of the square, the hotel that started it all in 1864 is still the grandest place to stay in Monaco, with chandelier-hung lobby, grand staircase and bedrooms and suites that remain firmly in the spirit of another age. It is home to the ever fashionable Bar Américain, the gourmet Louis XV restaurant and with direct access to the Thermes Marins spa and gym.

Le Méridien Beach Plaza

22 avenue Princesse Grace, Monte-Carlo; tel: +377-93 30 98 80; www.lemeridien montecarlo.com; €€€€

Just east of Larvotto beach, the huge, modern Méridien Beach is very popular with the *nouveaux riches* from Russia and Eastern Europe. It boasts contemporary artworks in the lobby and a 24-hour restaurant, landscaped outdoor pool, indoor pool and private beach. Rooms in two towers offer 180° panoramas; many of the other rooms have balconies with sea views.

Menton

Hôtel Aiglon

7 avenue de la Madone; tel: 04 93 57 55 55; www.hotelaiglon.net; €€

A 19th-century white stucco mansion converted into an atmospheric hotel with beautiful architectural details. The Belle Époque bar/salon is a delight; rooms are less elaborate, with a certain old-fashioned charm. Set in large gardens, there is an outdoor pool and a warm welcome for kids with a play area and ping pong.

Hôtel Lemon

10 rue Albert 1er; tel: 04 93 28 63 63; www.hotel-lemon.com; €

Eco-aware contemporary budget hotel in a Belle Epoque villa. Rooms are light and airy with 'breatheasy' paint; breakfast is made with local and organic produce. A breath of fresh air in staid Menton.

Hôtel Napoléon

29 Porte de France; tel: 04 93 35 89 50; www.napoleon-menton.com; €€

This modern seafront hotel near the Val Rahmeh Botanical Gardens offers sleekly

Clean lines at the Royal Antibes

furnished rooms and suites decked out in a palette of warm colours. Bedrooms at the front have generous balconies overlooking the Garavan Bay; those at the rear have mountain views. There is a bar, garden and outdoor pool and gym.

Hôtel Palm Garavan

3 avenue Porte de France; tel: 04 93 78 80 67; www.hotel-menton-garavan.com; €€
Opposite the beaches of Garavan Bay, this hotel has 19 contemporary-design rooms, some of which have balconies overlooking the sea and mountains; the others overlook the courtyard garden. There is free Wifi, one room with disabled access and parking available for a fee.

Riva Hotel

600 promenade du Soleil; tel: 04 92 10 92 10; www.rivahotel.com; €€
This three-star hotel on the seafront has been redecorated in contemporary style with a mix of bright colours and designer furniture. The selling points here are a spa with beauty treatments, an art gallery and a tea room.

Vence

Château St-Martin

route de Coursegoules; tel: 04 93 58 02 02; www.chateau-st-martin.com; €€€€
True luxury in the former castle of the Knights Templar, on the hills above Vence with views to the coast. Rooms are classic and the restaurant has an excellent reputation. The extensive grounds include tennis court and infinity pool. The

award-winning spa uses upmarket La Prairie products.

Hôtel Diana

79 avenue des Poilus; tel: 04 93 58 28 56; www.hotel-diana.fr; €€
This modern hotel on the edge of the Old Town has been tastefully redecorated after a change of ownership in 2007. Some of the pleasant rooms have a kitchenette and there's a large roof terrace with deckchairs, jacuzzi and exercise machines.

La Maison du Frêne

1 place du Frêne; tel: 04 93 24 37 83; www.lamaisondufrene.com; €€
This imposing 18th-century house has been turned into a temple of contemporary art where bright colours reign supreme and copies of Warhol and Picasso adorn the walls. The four rooms are very stylishly decorated and it's unlikely you'll want to leave.

Mas de Vence

539 avenue Emile Hugues; tel: 04 93 58 06 16; http://masdevence.azurline.com; €€
This modern neo-Provençal *mas* (farmhouse) located a 10-minute (uphill) walk from the town centre has a distinctly 1980s aura but is well maintained with decent-sized rooms (and efficient aircon), a restaurant serving Provençal specialities and staff who will go out of their way to help or inform. There is a good-sized swimming pool and a garden of terraced olive trees.

The lobby at the Royal Antibes   *The Royal Antibes' sleek café*

Antibes

Hôtel Eden

16 avenue Louis Gallet, Juan-les-Pins;
tel: 04 93 61 05 20; www.edenhoteljuan.
com; €€

About 15-minutes' walk from Antibes, this two-star hotel provides excellent budget accommodation. The family-run hotel is decorated in traditional Provençal style and breakfast is taken on the attractive, shaded terrace. Book a sea view if possible.

La Jabotte

13 avenue de Max Maurey, Antibes; tel: 04 93 61 45 89; www.jabotte.com; €€

Adorable – and affordable – lodgings with bright decor just up the street from the Plage de Salis. The original artwork in the 10 rooms is the work of one of the owners. There is a gorgeous garden patio and it's 15-minutes' walk from the beach.

Hôtel Mademoiselle

12 avenue Docteur Dautheville,
Juan-les-Pins; tel: 04 93 61 31 34;
www.hotelmademoisellejuan.com; €€

Hip hotel a stone's throw from the beach in Juan-les-Pins. Rooms are individually decorated in quirky style: think gold robots, dwarves and cushions with sleeping faces. Don't miss the tea room and its mouth-watering cakes. Bike hire is available.

Modern Hôtel

1 rue Fourmilière; tel: 04 92 90 59 05;
www.modernhotel06.com; €

Beyond its Art Deco pediment, this simple budget hotel won't win any prizes for style, but it is practical and well positioned in the pedestrianised part of the Old Town. Beds are comfortable and the spotless bathrooms have all been recently redone. There is air conditioning but no lift.

Hôtel Royal Antibes

16 boulevard Maréchal Leclerc, Antibes;
tel: 04 83 61 91 91; www.hotelroyal-
antibes.com; €€€

On the waterfront towards Cap d'Antibes, this modern luxury hotel, beach and spa opened its doors in 2011. The 63 rooms, suites and apartments offer the latest contemporary comforts and the New York-style Café Royal restaurant serves Mediterranean cuisine for breakfast, lunch and dinner.

Cannes

Hôtel 3.14

5 rue François Einesy; tel: 04 92 99 72 00;
www.3-14hotel.com; €€€

The most wittily over-the-top hotel in Cannes. The five floors of bedrooms are each themed after a different continent (America's style is Neo-Geo, Europe is influenced by the Moulin Rouge, etc), while Heaven is the landscaped rooftop pool and spa, and Earth, the sultry Oriental-style ground-floor salons and fashionable Mediterranean restaurant. There is also the 3.14 Beach restaurant for summer lunches.

Luxury suite, Five Seas Hotel

Hôtel 7 Art

23 rue du Maréchal Joffre; tel: 04 93 68 66 66; www.hotel-7art.com; €€

Bright and breezy budget boutique hotel which pays homage to the '7th art' aka cinema. Rooms are small but include free Wi-Fi and it's a short walk to the train station. If it's full, they also have two apartments near the Palais des Festivals.

Hôtel Les Allées

6 rue Emile Négrin; tel: 04 93 39 53 90; www.hotel-des-allees.com; €€

Highly recommended budget hotel in the heart of the pedestrian area. The colourful, contemporary, individually decorated rooms have air-conditioning, free Wifi and safes; some have balconies overlooking the port. Children under the age of six can stay for free.

Hôtel Canberra

120 rue d'Antibes; tel: 04 97 06 95 00; www.hotel-cannes-canberra.com; €€€

A smart, comfortable boutique hotel with 30 rooms and 5 suites. There is a pleasant outdoor pool and Le Café Blanc, a 1950s-style lounge bar and restaurant where snacks and tapas are available.

Hôtel Cavendish

11 boulevard Carnot; tel: 04 97 06 26 00; www.cavendish-cannes.com; €€

A characterful boutique hotel in an attractive Belle Époque building on the big boulevard that leads towards La Croisette. The comfortable period townhouse style was conceived by decora-

tor Christophe Tollemer as a homage to the English lords who once frequented the coast, with some wonderful circular rooms in the corner turret.

Hôtel Château de la Tour

10 avenue Font-de-Veyre, La Bocca; tel: 04 93 90 52 52; www.hotelchateaudelatour. com; €€

Hidden on the hill above the Plage du Midi, this is a rare place where you can capture a taste of the aristocratic villa lifestyle; the original wing complete with crenellated turret was built for a countess in the 1880s. The traditional rooms are comfortable and the restaurant, which is open to non-residents, moves out into the exotically planted garden in summer, where there is also an outdoor pool.

Five Seas Hotel

1 rue Notre Dame; tel: 04 63 36 05 05; www.five-seas-hotel-cannes.com; €€€€

The latest addition to Cannes' collection of luxury boutique hotels doesn't disappoint. The 45 rooms and suites have achingly hip design; the presidential suite has a terrace jacuzzi. There is also a fashionable restaurant, a Carita spa, a rooftop pool and a yacht available for guests to book.

Hôtel Florian

8 rue du Commandant André; tel: 04 93 39 24 82; www.hotel-leflorian.fr; €

On the hippest shopping street, this is one of the best budget options in town. There are 20 rooms and 15 apartments

sleeping up to four people. With plenty of bars in the vicinity, it's reassuring that there is double glazing and aircon.

Le Mistral Hôtel

13 rue des Belges; tel: 04 93 39 91 46; www.mistral-hotel.com; €

This is a stylish budget discovery in a simple blue-shuttered building just a couple of streets back from the Palais des Festivals. The 10 rooms, named after different winds (chinook, sirocco, etc), are comfortably decked out in warm colours and stripey wood; bigger ones can accommodate three people and have bathrooms with windows. No lift.

Hôtel Molière

5 rue Molière; tel: 04 93 38 16 16; www.hotel-moliere.com; €€

There is a relaxed mood at this small, well-located contemporary design hotel, set at the rear of a long, flowery garden between La Croisette and rue d'Antibes. The 24 rooms sport modern minimalist tones, most with good-sized balconies. Enjoy breakfast in the garden in summer.

Hôtel Splendid

4–6 rue Félix Faure; tel: 04 97 06 22 22; www.splendid-hotel-cannes.com; €€

A sparkling white Belle Époque edifice ideally situated in the heart of the action, near the port and almost opposite the Palais des Festivals. Rooms have been comfortably updated while retaining period flourishes. Breakfast is served on a large sunny terrace.

St-Tropez

La Ferme d'Augustin

Plage de Tahiti, Ramatuelle; tel: 04 94 55 97 00; www.fermeaugustin.com; €€€€

Set in vineyards next to Tahiti Beach, this family-run hotel in a lovely old farmhouse is surrounded by luxuriant gardens. The bedrooms overlook the gardens and many have balconies and sea views. The guests-only restaurant uses produce from the hotel's own kitchen garden. There's a heated swimming pool and secure parking. Most guests are regulars, so reserve well ahead. Closed mid-October–March.

Kon-Tiki Village

Plage de Pampelonne; www.riviera-villages.com; €€

Not strictly camping, but Tahitian-style huts which sleep up to six people and some chalets right on the beach. There are several restaurants, a spa and a whole host of activities so it's a great place for families. The company also has two other parks in the area, Prairies de la Mer and Toison d'Or.

Hôtel des Lices

10 avenue Augustin Grangeon; tel: 04 97 28 28; www.hoteldeslices.com; €€€€

Traditional three-star hotel with 40 comfortable, modern rooms, some of which overlook the garden and pool (the poolside bar is a popular spot for cocktails). Next door is a pristine villa for rent which sleeps up to seven people in three rooms. No restaurant.

Hôtel Lou Cagnard

18 avenue Paul Roussell; tel: 04 94 97 04 24; www.hotel-lou-cagnard.com; €€
This old Provençal house is the best of the 'budget' accommodation in St-Tropez. Its 19 rooms are simply decorated and breakfast under the fig trees in the garden is a delight. There isn't a restaurant or pool but there is free parking.

Hôtel Pastis

75 avenue du Général Leclerc; tel: 04 98 12 56 50; www.pastis-st-tropez.com; €€€€
This is more like a dream home than a hotel. The nine individually decorated rooms overlook a courtyard with a swimming pool; each boasts artworks from the owners' Pop Art collection; one room has a copper bathtub. A special place.

Hôtel Les Palmiers

26 boulevard Vasserot; tel: 04 94 97 01 61; www.hotel-les-palmiers.com; €€
Proof that good-value no-frills accommodation exists in St-Tropez, Les Palmiers has a great location on place des Lices, although the hotel itself is set back in a garden with palms and orange trees, where you can eat breakfast or have an evening drink. Rooms are simple but clean, with Provençal fabrics and modern paintings.

Kube Hotel St-Tropez

Route de St-Tropez (D98), Gassin; tel: 04 94 97 20 00; www.kubehotel.com; €€€€
This offshoot of the trendy Paris Kube has kept the trademark glass-and-steel reception cube and ice bar where you drink vodka shots in sub-zero temperatures, but combines it all with more of a resorty feel. A gorgeous pool stretches out in front of the hotel between shady lawns where you can eat in summer. There's also a smaller heated pool at the rear, outdoor cocktail bar, an indoor lounge bar and a rooftop Champagne bar where you can listen to the DJ or settle in a sofa on fake grass. Bedrooms are suave exercises in grey and white with plenty of witty touches.

La Mistralée

1 avenue du Général Leclerc; tel: 04 98 12 91 12; www.hotel-mistralee.com; €€€€
This white 19th-century villa near the port used to belong to Alexandre 'hairdresser to the stars' de Paris, but is now a sophisticated small hotel, with a boudoir-style conservatory lounge, an outdoor pool in the walled garden and a restaurant where the chef will personally concoct your menu. Each of the 11 rooms has a different theme, ranging from colourful 'chinoise' to manly brown and white-striped Hemingway.

Massif des Maures

45 boulevard des Pêcheurs

Super-Lavandou, Le Lavandou; tel: 04 94 71 46 02; www.chambrehotes-draganja.com; €
One bedroom with its own private terrace in the hosts' curved, modern villa about 15-minutes' walk from the town

centre; there is also an apartment available to rent. Hire a bike to explore the area or relax by the pool in the luxuriant garden. Due to its elevated position, there are uninterrupted views over the coast.

Hôtel Bailli de Suffren

Avenue des Américains, Le Rayol Canadel; tel: 04 98 04 47 00; www.lebaillide suffren.com; €€€

Located on a secluded beach beneath the Domaine de Rayol Gardens, this curved 1960s building – all rooms have balconies or terraces and sea views – has been pleasantly refurbished in a modern, Provençal-chic style, with a heated pool, private beach, bar, gastronomic and poolside restaurants and boats for hire. Closed mid-October–mid-April.

Hôtel Baptistin

quai Baptistin Pins, Le Lavandou; tel: 04 98 00 44 51; www.baptistin-hotel-lavandou.com; €€

A modern hotel with just 14 stylishly decorated rooms opposite the port and surrounded by pines and palm trees. The sea-view rooms all have balconies with seats. No restaurant.

Hôtel Notre Dame

15 avenue de la Libération, Collobrières; tel: 04 94 48 07 13; www.hotel-notre-dame.eu; €€

Charming, attractive hotel housed in an 18th-century coaching inn with 10 rooms decorated in a modern, Provençal style.

The restaurant serves market-inspired dishes and there is an outdoor pool.

Hôtel de la Plage

boulevard de la Plage, La Favière, Bormes-les-Mimosas; tel: 04 94 71 02 74; www.hotelbormes.com; €€

This family-oriented hotel in Bormes' beach resort of La Favière has been run by the same family since it opened in 1939. Most of the 45 air-conditioned rooms have balconies or terraces, and there's a restaurant serving dinner if desired. *Pétanque* and ping pong outside. Closed Oct–Easter.

Hôtel Restaurant Bellevue

14 place Gambetta, Bormes-les-Mimosas; tel: 04 94 71 15 15; www.bellevuebormes.com; €

This friendly village hotel/restaurant has attractively redecorated its 17 bedrooms and added air conditioning, yet kept its prices remarkably low. Some rooms give onto animated place Gambetta, but the best have a *belle vue* from its hilltop perch to the coast.

Le Verger Maelvi

route de Collobrières, Grimaud; tel: 04 94 55 57 80; www.hotel-grimaud.com; €€

On the edge of the village, this traditional Provençal house, which was completely renovated in 2011, is the perfect place to get away from it all. The 14 rooms have contemporary décor and there's a lovely swimming pool. No restaurant.

RESTAURANTS

The French Riviera has restaurants to suit all styles, budgets and occasions, ranging from formal gastronomic affairs and inventive modern restaurants to trendy see-and-be-seen beach haunts and the traditional everyday bistro. Restaurants in Vieux Nice and Cannes' Le Suquet mainly serve age-old Niçois and Provençal specialities, while fish restaurants tend to be concentrated around the ports. Fusion cuisine is fashionable in St-Tropez and there are numerous Italian restaurants towards the frontier in Villefranche, Monaco and Menton. Top restaurants may need reserving weeks ahead, but it is always worth ringing at the last minute to see if there is a table. At other restaurants, try to call before going, especially at weekends and during the tourist season.

Nice

Auberge de Théo

52 avenue Cap de Croix; tel: 04 93 81 26 19; Tue–Sat L and D, €€

This cheerful family-run Italian trattoria, with an amusing rustic decor of hay-racks, farm implements and Neopolitan crib figures, is one of the rare restaurants in Cimiez. Authentic dishes include mixed antipasti, pasta with swordfish, beef tagliatelle and little rum babas doused in limoncello.

Le Bistro Gourmand

3 rue Desboutin; tel: 04 92 14 55 55; Tue–Sat L and D (closed Wed lunch, Sat lunch and all day Sun); €€€

At the western edge of the old town, this stylish modern restaurant offers excellent-value market-inspired Michelin-star Mediterranean cuisine with a lunch menu starting at €23. The wine list includes local AOC Bellet.

Comptoir du Marché

8 rue du Marché; tel: 04 93 13 45 01; D Tue–Sat L and D; €€

The retro dining room in the latest enterprise by Arnaud Crespo of Le Bistrot d'Antoine is usually packed to the rafters with arty sorts and lawyers from the nearby court. There's a limited-but-tasty range of dishes and a good wine list. Book in advance.

Keisuke Matsushima

22ter rue de France; tel: 04 93 82 26 06; www.keisukematsushima.com; Tue–Fri L and D, Sat D; €€€

Japan meets Provence with brilliant young chef Keisuke Matsushima, who

---

Price guide for a three-course dinner for one, not including wine:

€€€€ = over 60 euros
€€€ = 40–60 euros
€€ = 25–40 euros
€ = below 25 euros

The open kitchen at Joël Robuchon Monte–Carlo

trained with some of France's top chefs to become one of Nice's gastronomic success stories. Subtly lit slate tables and geometrical lines provide a suitable setting for his artistically presented creations; think green, purple and wild asparagus with lemon froth or scallops with truffles, peas and wasabi.

Luc Salsedo

14 rue Maccarrani; tel: 04 93 82 24 12; www.restaurant-salsedo.com;Thu–Tue D; €€€
After working at Le Louis XV in Monaco and Chèvre d'Or in Èze, among other top restaurants, Ducasse alumnus Salsedo set up on his own with an adventurous contemporary menu that changes every 10 days. The setting is a rather dressed-up dining room in the New Town. He offers cookery classes too.

La Maison de Marie

5 rue Masséna; tel: 04 93 82 15 93; www.la maisondemarie.com; daily L and D; €€
Set back from the frenetic scrum of pedestrianised rue Masséna, La Maison de Marie offers a bit more sophistication than the nearby brasseries and pizzerias, with candlelit tables in an attractive cobbled courtyard or in the elegant dining room. A stylish take on French and Mediterranean favourites ranges from foie gras, stuffed sardines and herb-encrusted lamb to pasta with scampi.

La Merenda

4 rue Raoul Bosio; no phone; Mon–Fri L and D; €€
No telephone, no credit cards and the sheer difficulty of getting a table – you have to come by before to reserve one – are all part of the Merenda mystique. That and a reputation for some of the most authentic local specialities in town, prepared by chef Dominique de Stanc, who gave up a post at the grandiose Chantecler for this tiny elbow-to-elbow bistro in Vieux Nice, packing in an international set of foodies for hearty dishes like courgette flower fritters, stuffed sardines, *daube de boeuf* and *tarte au citron*.

Les Pêcheurs

18 quai des Docks; tel: 04 93 89 59 61; Wed–Sun L and D; €€
Smart port-side restaurant with a canopied terrace where, unsurprisingly given its name ('The Fishermen'), fish is the speciality. The cuisine sometimes has a touch of the Far East such as pan-seared tuna Teriyaki with stir-fried vegetables.

L'Univers de Christian Plumail

54 boulevard Jean Jaurès; tel: 04 93 62 32 22; www.christian-plumail.com; Mon D, Tue–Fri and Sun L and D, Sat D; €€€
Although it looks unassuming from the exterior, L'Univers is one of Nice's very top gourmet destinations for the exquisite modern southern cuisine by Christian Plumail, which changes frequently according to the catch and the market produce of the day. Choose from four value-for-money set menus or splurge on the creative à la carte.

The Corniches

African Queen

Port de Plaisance, Beaulieu-sur-Mer; tel: 04 93 01 10 85; www.africanqueen.fr; daily L and D; €€€

Frequented by celebrities and rich Russians, this restaurant overlooking the marina is probably past its prime but worth going to for the people watching. The food is mainly Italian but they've introduced a Japanese menu.

Café de la Fontaine

4 avenue du Général de Gaulle, La Turbie; tel: 04 93 28 52 79; summer daily L and D, winter Tue–Sun L and D; €€

Bruno Cirino of the acclaimed Hostellerie Jérôme took over the village café and turned it into a relaxed gourmet bistro, serving wonderful market-inspired regional cooking at remarkable prices. Reservations recommended.

La Cave Nature

17 rue Poilu, Villefranche-sur-Mer; tel: 09 84 38 15 09; Thu–Mon L and D, Wed D; €

This wine bar specialising in organic products offers platters of ham and cheese as well as open sandwiches to accompany your vino (the rosé is particularly popular). Desserts usually involve fresh fruit. Sit outside on a fine day and watch the world go by in the old town.

Paloma Beach

1 route de Sainte-Hospice, St-Jean-Cap-Ferrat; tel: 04 93 01 64 71; www.paloma-beach.com; Easter–Sept daily L and D; €€€

At the waters' edge, hidden from view, this chic beach restaurant is a favourite with Hollywood A-listers and rock stars. Admire the mega yachts in the bay as you tuck into fresh fish accompanied by a chilled rosé.

La Pinède

10 avenue Raymond Gramaglia, Cap d'Ail; tel: 04 93 78 37 10; www.restaurantla pinede.com; Mar–Oct Thu–Tue L and D; €€€

The waterside setting of this seafood restaurant makes it the perfect place for a romantic meal. Grilled salmon with champagne sauce is recommended as is the pasta with fresh lobster. A real treat.

Le Sloop

Port de Plaisance, St-Jean-Cap-Ferrat; tel: 04 93 01 48 63; Thu–Tue L and Mon, Thu–Sat D, closed mid-Nov–mid-Dec; €€€

Fish, shellfish and French classics are served in a maritime-themed dining room or on the terrace overlooking the yachting marina. This is a favourite eating place of Lord Lloyd-Webber and the late Michael Winner.

Monaco

Beef Bar

42 quai Jean-Charles Rey, Fontvieille; tel: 377-97 77 09 29; www.beefbar.com; daily L and D; €€€

Overlooking the yacht harbour in Fontvieille, this is a chic, modern canteen for carnivores that specialises in different cuts of beef – raw and grilled – from

different breeds, imported direct from Argentina, the Netherlands and the US.

Café Lorca

Grimaldi Forum, 10 avenue Princesse Grace; tel: 377-99 99 29 29; www.cafe llorca.com; Mon–Fri L; €

This chic, minimalist bistro on the first floor of the Grimaldi Forum, is a more accessible offering from acclaimed chef Alain Llorca, formerly of the Moulin de Mougins. The menu focuses on Mediterranean flavours and dishes.

Joël Robuchon Monte-Carlo

Hôtel Métropole, 4 avenue de la Madone, Monte-Carlo; tel: 377-93 15 15 10; www.metropole.com; Thu–Tue L and D; €€€€

Joël Robuchon has exported his luxury tapas formula from Paris to Monaco with everything prepared in an open kitchen by emissary Christophe Cussac. Dine on a variety of beautifully prepared, inventive mini-dishes, such as foie gras with apricots, artichokes with squid and chorizo, and caramelised quail, in a cossetted dining room decorated by Jacques Garcia.

Loga

25 boulevard des Moulins, Monte-Carlo; tel: 377 93 30 87 72; Mon–Sat L and Thu–Tue D; €€

A busy, convivial Italian bistro and tea room in the heart of the shopping district. Specialities include *escalope milanaise* (fried breaded veal cutlet) and homemade *tiramisu* and there also are *barbajuans*, a local speciality which is a kind of deep-fried spinach and ricotta pasty, on the menu. Stop by for tea and cake in the afternoon.

Le Louis XV

Hôtel de Paris, place du Casino, Monte-Carlo; tel: 377-98 06 88 64; www.alain-ducasse.com; Sept–mid-Nov and Jan–June Thur–Mon L and D, July–Aug also Wed D; €€€€

One of the most glamorous restaurants in Europe, with sumptuous decor and immaculate service. Ducasse's acclaimed cuisine is now handled by protégé Franck Cerutti, taking Mediterranean cooking to the heights of haute cuisine. Leave room for the local strawberries with mascarpone ice cream.

La Note Bleue

Plage Larvotto, avenue Princesse Grace; tel: 377-93 50 05 02; www.lanotebleue. mc; mid-May–mid-Sept daily L and D, mid-Mar–mid-May and mid-Sept–mid-Dec daily L; €€€

An excellent beach restaurant with stylish decor is a relaxed place for lunching on well-prepared modern Mediterranean-wide dishes, including plenty of grilled fish. On summer weekends there are free jazz concerts in the evening from quality ensembles.

Polpetta

2 rue Paradis, Monte-Carlo; tel: 377 93 50 67 84; www.restaurantpolpetta.com;

Mauro Colagreco at work at Mirazur

Sun–Fri L and D, Sat D; €€
Once frequented by Frank Sinatra and Prince Rainier, this bistro offers hearty Italian food, and is among the best value for money in Monaco. Specialities include fresh fish, veal, homemade pasta and truffle-based dishes.

Stars 'n' Bars

6 quai Antoine 1er; tel: 377-97 97 95 95; www.starsnbars.com; L and D daily; €€
Burgers and Tex-Mex are the name of the game at this hugely popular American restaurant, which has racing cars hanging from the ceiling and a huge terrace overlooking Port Hercule. There is a friendly welcome for all, from small children to racing drivers and pop stars. Food is served all day.

St-Benoît

10 ter avenue de la Costa; tel: 377 93 25 02 34; Tue–Sun L and Tue–Sat D; €€€
A favourite with locals, this smart restaurant overlooks the port. The emphasis is on classic fish and shellfish with the menu featuring the likes of prawn skewer with mushroom cream but there's also steak with garlic and anchovy sauce.

Le Tip Top

11 avenue des Spélugues; tel: 377-93 50 69 13; daily L and D; €
A jovial, old-fashioned restaurant and bar that surprisingly still exists in Monte-Carlo, feeding steak and matchstick chips, spaghetti and pizzas to local workers at lunch and to absolutely everyone (including Prince Albert) in the dead of night.

Valentin

Galerie du Park Palace, 27 avenue de la Costa; tel: 377 93 50 60 00; www.valentin.mc; Mon–Fri B and D; €
Cool but cosy Italian restaurant in an upmarket shopping mall a short walk north of the casino. The menu changes daily and includes the likes of stuffed courgette flowers with frittata and cheese. Leave room for a dessert.

Menton

Le Bruit Qui Court

31 quai Bonaparte; tel: 04 93 35 94 64; daily D; €€
On the quayside beneath the old town and overlooking the port, the terrace of this 'semi-gastronomic' restaurant is a pleasant place to spend a mealtime. On the menu are the usual meat and fish dishes but they do a mean scampi risotto too. The Menton lemon tart is recommended.

Le 5

Hotel Mediterranée, 5 rue de la République; tel: 04 92 41 81 81; www.hotel-med-menton.com; daily B, L and D; €€
A modern restaurant in a three-star hotel with an excellent-value two-course set lunch menu (€13) and a choice of three *plats du jour*. Food is a mix of Provençal and Mediterranean and there are some delicious lemon-based desserts.

Superbly presented pigeon dish at Mirazur

Crocantine

3 rue Trenca; tel: 04 93 51 85 62; Tue–Sat
L and D; €

This little restaurant creates its dishes
with produce from Les Halles, which
are opposite. Most of the offerings are
vegetable based and the salads are the
main reason to come here. However,
there are also burgers, omelettes and
tartare on the menu.

Mirazur

30 avenue Aristide Briand; tel: 04 92 41
86 86; www.mirazur.fr; July–Aug Thu–Sun
L and daily D, Sept–June Wed–Sun L and
D; €€€€

With adventurous Argentine chef Mauro
Colagreco at the helm, Menton now has
one of the most exciting restaurants on
the coast. Daring combinations of the finest ingredients, including fruit and vegetables from the kitchen garden, meet
impeccable technique in specialities like
lowtemperature pigeons. It is all served
up in a modern dining room near the Italian border, with views over the bay.

Restaurant L'Ulivo

21 place du Cap; tel: 04 93 35 45 65;
www.restaurant-ulivo.com; Tue–Sat L and
D, Sun L; €€

Occupying a listed building on a pretty
square, this restaurant offers well-prepared Sardinian specialities, including vegetable antipasti, roast suckling
pig, plump stuffed pasta, octopus and
mountain ham and liqueurs made from
myrtle.

Vence

Les Bacchanales

247 avenue de Provence; tel: 04 93 24 19
19; www.lesbacchanales.com; Thur–Mon L
and D; €€€

In 2008, Christophe Dufau moved from
his discreet restaurant in Tourettes-sur-
Loup to a 19th-century villa located on
the edge of Vence towards the Matisse
Chapel. Beautiful, colourful dishes com-
bine fresh regional produce and a taste
for wild herbs and edible flowers. The
menu changes every week.

Antibes

La Cafetière Fêlée

18 rue du Marc; tel: 04 93 34 51 86; Tue–
Sat L and D; €€

Fusion cuisine is the name of the game
at this restaurant in the old town. Chef
Julien Fiengo, a graduate of the prestigious Escoffier school, serves up the
likes of Tandoori scallops or duck breast
glazed with truffle-flavoured honey in
the stone-walled dining room.

La Passion des Mets

7 rue James Close, tel: 04 92 94 07 31;
daily D; €

This stylish restaurant with very friendly
service in Vieil Antibes draws a well-
dressed, mainly French clientele. The
speciality is generous main-course woks
of sautéed beef, noodles and fresh vegetables, but you will also find other
French and world flavours, such as a
good risotto, foie gras, Thai salad and
Toblerone mousse.

La Bastide Saint-Antoine in Grasse

La Taverne du Safranier

1 place du Safranier; tel: 04 93 34 80 50; July and Aug Mon and Tue D, Wed–Sun L and D, Sept, Oct and Mar–June Tue–Sat L and D, Sun L; €€

This convivial bistro with tables on a square in the Quartier du Safranier is a stalwart of the Commune and very popular with arty locals. Well-prepared regional dishes include *aioli*, grilled red pepper salad, marinated sardines, ravioli, the fresh fish of the day and a gigantic lemon meringue tart.

Les Vieux Murs

25 promenade Amiral de Grasse; tel: 04 93 34 06 73; www.lesvieuxmurs.com; daily L and D; €€€

Les Vieux Murs is a chic restaurant located in stylish vaulted rooms in the port's old ramparts, which gained a new chef Stéphane Arnal and a new Venetian-inspired decor in 2009. There is a choice of Mediterranean set menu or grander French classics à la carte.

Cannes

Aux Bons Enfants

80 rue Meynadier; no tel; Mon–Sat L and D; €

A simple bistro located near to the market, which has been in the same family since 1934 and serves up comforting regional home cooking, such as grilled sardines and herby Sisteron lamb accompanied with courgettes or Swiss chard. No credit cards.

Belle Plage

Boulevard Jean Hibert; tel: 04 93 38 84 39; www.belleplage.net; summer daily B and L, winter Thu–Tue; €€

West of the port, this beach restaurant offers the best value-for-money food on the waterfront. Start with a salad, move on to grilled sea bass with fennel then finish off with some profiteroles. There are sun loungers for hire if you want to make an afternoon of it.

Mantel

22 rue St-Antoine; tel: 04 93 39 13 10; www.restaurantmantel.com; Sept–June Thur D, Fri–Tue L and D, July–Aug daily D; €€

This sleek dining room in a bright yellow house in the Old Town is an acclaimed address for gourmet southern cooking. Chef Noël Mantel, whose pedigree includes the Negresco and Le Louis XV, mixes tradition and modernity in dishes such as stuffed vegetables, courgette flower fritters, rabbit with thyme and polenta and fish baked in sea salt.

Le Relais des Semailles

9–11 rue St-Antoine; tel: 04 93 39 22 32; Mar–Jan Mon D, Tue–Sat L and D, Sun L; €€

White linen, beams and exposed stone walls provide a pretty setting at this upmarket bistro in Le Suquet, where the emphasis is on fine seasonal ingredients. Modern Provençal dishes might include grilled squid in frothy seafood sauce and roast veal

Seafood dish at La Bastide *The dining room at La Bastide*

with artichokes. There is a good, if pricey, wine list.

New York New York

1 allée de la Liberté; tel: 04 93 06 78 27; www.nynycannes.com; daily B, L, D; €€€
This fashionable New York-loft style bar and restaurant opposite the Palais des Festivals offers excellent pizzas, salads, burgers and grilled meats – among many other dishes. As it's part of the Baoli Group (the coolest club in town), there is a lounge bar with good music.

Sea Sens

Five Seas Hotel, 1 rue Notre Dame; tel: 04 63 36 05 06; www.five-seas-hotel-cannes. com; Tue–Sat D; €€€€
Hip Michelin-star restaurant on the fifth floor (great views) of an ultra-cool new hotel where Arnaud Tabarec's flavours take diners on a trip around the world. Leave room for dessert – they're made by the World Pastry Champion.

Le Restaurant Arménien

82 La Croisette; tel: 04 93 94 00 58; www.lerestaurantarmenien.com; summer daily D, winter Tue–Sun D; €€€
What claims to be the only authentic Armenian restaurant on the Côte d'Azur is the place to discover this cuisine that resembles the eastern Mediterranean cooking of Greece, Turkey and the Lebanon. Feast on a table full of different meze, such as stuffed vine leaves, hummous, aubergine purée and grilled kebabs.

Grasse

La Bastide Saint-Antoine

48 avenue Henri Dunant; tel: 04 93 70 94 94; www.jacques-chibois.com; daily L and D; €€€€
Grasse's gourmet treat is set in a lovely old olive grove outside the town centre, where you dine outside on the terrace in summer, and in the well-restored 18th-century *bastide* in winter. Chef Jacques Chibois puts his personal stamp on southern cuisine with dishes like foie gras with artichokes, succulent lamb with broad beans and fennel or a combination of purple and wild green asparagus; truffles and mushrooms are a speciality in winter.

St-Tropez

Brasserie des Arts

5 place des Lices; 04 94 40 27 37; www.brasseriedesarts.com; daily L and D; €€
The 'BA' offers people-watching on the terrace overlooking place des Lices, and sofas and padded walls for a more party ambience inside. The menu ranges from fashionable carpaccios, risottos and crumbles to classic steak tartare, fish with olives and herby lamb, as well as brunch on Sunday. Dress up to look as cool as the staff. Food is served until midnight in peak season; the bar opens until 2am or later.

Le Girelier

Quai Jean Jaurès; tel: 04 94 97 03 87; www.legirelier.fr; daily L and D; €€

Bouillabaisse reinvented at La Vague d'Or

Thanks to the efforts of designer Kristian Gavoille, this ever-fashionable harbourside fish and shellfish restaurant has gained a chic fisherman's-shack-inspired decor following a change of ownership. Fish and prawns *à la plancha* (cooked on a metal plate) are a speciality here, along with Le Girelier's own take on bouillabaisse.

Senequier

Quai Jean Jaurès; tel: 04 94 97 20 20; www.senequier.com; end-Feb–early Jan daily B, L and D; €€

This St-Tropez institution, which opened as a patisserie specialising in nougat in 1887 (still available at 4 place aux Herbes), has had a recent makeover but happily has kept the rows of red directors' chairs for surveying the portside scene. Not cheap but a must at aperitif time.

Le Quai

22 quai Jean Jaurès; tel: 04 94 97 04 07; daily L and D; €€€

This portside restaurant and nightclub offers fashionable Japanese and Indo-Chinese fusion (sushi, sashimi and wok dishes). Sit in white tub chairs and admire the yachts from the covered terrace or head inside to enjoy the cabaret and maybe some dancing.

La Vague d'Or

Hôtel Résidence de la Pinède, plage de la Bouillabaisse; tel: 04 94 55 91 00; www.residencepinede.com; Apr–Oct daily D; €€€€

In 2013, this gourmet restaurant won its third Michelin star, making it only the third restaurant in the Provence region to have this accolade. Expect to pay upwards of €120 to sample Arnaud Donckele's inspired Provençal cuisine such as turbot in a Camargue salt crust flavoured with lemongrass and seaweed.

La Voûte by BB

24 rue du Portail Neuf; tel: 04 94 54 32 76; daily L and D, closed Nov–Mar; €€

A small restaurant with a 1980s vibe which is a haven for carnivores in a fish-heavy region. On the menu you'll find cuts of the best beef: Kobe, Angus, Salers and Charolais but there's tapas too.

Massif des Maures

Restaurant de l'Estagnol

Parc de l'Estagnol, Bormes-les-Mimosas; tel: 04 94 64 71 11; Apr–Sept daily L and D; €€

Alfresco eating under the pines, set just back from the beach at l'Estagnol. The speciality is fresh fish and langoustines grilled on an open wood fire; try them with spaghetti. Bouillabaisse is also on the menu.

La Farigoulette

Rue Victor Léon, Ramatuelle; tel: 04 94 79 20 49; Apr–June and Sept daily L and D, July–Aug daily D; €€

This simple, informal bistro has tables in an ancient stone-walled room or

Waterside dining

Three-Michelin-star dish at La Vague d'Or

out on the pavement. Come for grilled meats and satisfying traditional southern favourites, such as an intense, herby *daube de boeuf*, *anchoïade* and pasta dishes.

Lou Portaou

1 rue Cubert des Poètes, Bormes-les-Mimosas; tel: 04 94 64 86 37; mid-Dec–mid-Nov Tue, Sat D, Wed–Thur and Sun–Mon L and D; €€

This restaurant has a wonderfully atmospheric setting in a fortified medieval tower which is hung with medieval-style knick-knacks. The menu here features Provençal dishes with an original touch, including tapas, as well as a good selection of local Côtes de Provence wines.

Hôtel-Restaurant Des Maures

19 boulevard Lazare Carnot, Collobrières; tel: 04 94 48 07 10; daily L and D; €

A popular, unpretentious, family-run restaurant with tables on the terrace spanning the Réal Collobrier river. Sustaining rustic fare includes roast pork with figs.

La Rastègue

48 boulevard du Levant, Le Pin des Bormes; Tel: 04 94 15 19 41; Bormes-les-Mimosas; Thu–Sun L Tue–Sun D; €€

Creative Provençal cooking has earned young chef Jérôme Masson a Michelin star. Try roast pigeon breast in cocoa sauce washed down with a regional wine. The dining room is classy but the views from the terrace are stunning.

Les Tamaris 'Chez Raymond'

Plage de St-Clair, Le Lavandou; tel: 04 94 71 02 70; Wed–Mon L (winter only) and daily D (June–Sept only), Closed Nov–Feb; €€€

The most upmarket of the fish restaurants along the Plage de St-Clair is renowned for its bourride and the excellent daily catch. The service can be patchy but it's worth going there for the good food and relaxed French Riviera vibe.

La Tonnelle

23 place Gambetta, Bormes-les-Mimosas; tel: 04 94 71 34 84; www.la-tonnelle-bormes.com; July and Aug daily D, May, June and Sept Fri–Tue L and D, Thur D, Oct–mid Nov and mid-Dec–Apr Fri–Tue L and D; €€

In a stylish dining room on Bormes' main square, chef Gil Renard cooks up superb modern Provençal fare, combining regional produce with a well-judged use of spices.

La Verdoyante

866 chemin vicinal Coste-Brigade, Gassin; tel: 04 94 56 16 23. Open Tue, Thu–Sun L and Thu–Mon D, closed Nov–Jan; €€

Inspired by the vegetables and herbs of Provence, Laurent Mouret's traditional cuisine is served in the idyllic surroundings of his family's farmhouse. Try the goat's cheese with crushed olives for dessert. You can see the Bay of St-Tropez from the terrace.

Le Croisette Casino Barrière

NIGHTLIFE

The Riviera's cultural programme is strongly concentrated on Nice, and to a lesser extent Monaco, while St-Tropez and Cannes lean more towards clubbing. Nightclubs will often describe themselves as '*club privé*', meaning they can pick and choose who they let in; there are also plenty of less elitist DJ bars, though.

Music and Dance Venues

Opéra de Nice

4 rue St-Francis-de-Paule, Nice; tel: 04 92 17 40 00; www.opera-nice.org
Nice's ornate opera house was entirely rebuilt in the 1880s, according to plans approved by Charles Garnier, after the old Italian theatre caught fire during the overture of *Lucia di Lammermoor* in 1881. It is used for opera, ballet and symphony concerts, with an emphasis on popular opera classics.

Palais Nikaia

163 route de Grenoble, Nice; tel: 04 92 29 31 29; www.nikaia.fr
Nice's big stadium venue can seat over 6,000 in its indoors configuration and stand up to 52,000 in its open-air version, so this is the place for farewell tours and comebacks by rock giants like Johnny Hallyday, the Rolling Stones or U2, along with crowd-pulling musicals and stars of the stand-up comedy circuit.

Salle Garnier

Place du Casino, Monaco; tel: +377-98 06 28 28; www.opera.mc
Designed by Charles Garnier, Monte-Carlo's sumptuous opera house was added onto the casino building in 1879 to encourage gamblers to stay in town longer; it has a prestigious history of opera and ballet premieres, and often features big-name soloists.

Théâtre de Grasse

2 rue Maximin Isnard, Grasse; tel: 04 93 40 53 00; www.theatredegrasse.com
A striking modern venue that puts on a multidisciplinary mix of dance, theatre, circus and music from visiting companies that are usually in town for just a night or two. Closed August.

Théâtre Lino Ventura

168 boulevard de l'Ariane, Nice; tel: 04 97 00 10 70; www.tlv-nice.org
Since opening in 1992, the 700-capacity Lino Ventura has proved to be one of the most dynamic venues in Nice, showcasing a broad spectrum of current rock and pop trends from international names and local groups, along with circus and contemporary dance.

Theatres and Cinemas

Cinémathèque de Nice

Acropolis, 3 esplanade Kennedy, Nice; tel: 04 92 04 06 66; www.cinematheque-

nice.com
The offshoot of the Paris Cinémathèque screens both classic and more recent movies in themed seasons and retrospectives of great actors and directors.

Théâtre Antibea

15 rue Georges Clémenceau, Antibes; tel: 04 93 34 24 30; www.theatre-antibea.com
This 120-seat theatre on the site of an old chapel puts on a varied and energetic programme ranging from Racine and other French classics to modern European drama, including occasional pieces in English.

Théâtre National de Nice

Promenade des Arts, Nice; tel: 04 93 13 90 90; www.tnn.fr
The region's most important venue for contemporary drama is renowned for premiering new plays both by visiting companies and by its own troupe directed by Daniel Benoin.

Nightclubs and Casinos

Le Bâoli

Port Canto, La Croisette, Cannes; tel: 04 93 43 03 43; www.lebaoli.com
This all-night restaurant, sushi bar and discothèque with a tented Arabian Nights and palm trees setting draws a VIP crowd and Cannes' gilded youth.

Casino Ruhl

1 promenade des Anglais, Nice; tel: 04 97 03 12 22; www.lucienbarriere.com
Where gambling combines with glitz:

Baccarat chandeliers, gaming tables, 300 slot machines, plus a cabaret revue at weekends.

Le Croisette Casino Barrière

Palais des Festivals, Cannes; tel: 04 92 98 78 00, www.lucienbarriere.com
A panoply of roulette, black jack and other table games, poker and slot machines in the heart of the Palais des Festivals, with a brasserie overlooking the port.

Les Marches

Palais des Festivals, Cannes; tel: 04 93 39 77 21; www.lesmarches-club.com
On the first floor of the legendary Palais des Festivals, this fashionable club which attracts top DJs overlooks the harbour. The terrace is the perfect place for a sunset cocktail.

Papagayo

Résidence du Port, St-Tropez; tel: 04 94 97 95 95.
St-Tropez's party people have flocked to this two-level club by the port for more than 40 years. Closed mid-Nov–mid-Feb.

La Siesta

Route du Bord de Mer, Antibes; tel: 04 93 33 31 31; www.joa-casino.com
This big, brash seafront complex on the eastern edge of Antibes spans the casino/club/restaurant spectrum including a vast open-air beach disco in summer and a refreshingly unpretentious attitude compared to some of its snootier rivals.

Monaco Aquarium

A–Z

A

Age Restrictions

Minimum ages: consent 15, marriage 18, buying alcohol 16, drinking wine or beer in a bar 16, drinking spirits in a bar 18, driving 18.

B

Budgeting

Expect to pay €3.50 for a 25cl *(un demi)* of draught lager and €4–7 for a glass of house wine. A main course in a budget restaurant will cost €10–15, in a moderate one €18–25 and in an expensive one €45–60. A double room in a cheap hotel will cost around €60–80, in a moderate one €120–160 and in a deluxe hotel €300. Prices are generally higher along the coast. A single bus ticket in Nice costs €1.50, a one-day bus pass €5.

C

Children

Most hotels have family rooms or suites that can sleep three or four, or can add a folding bed in a double room. Children are always accepted in restaurants; children's menus – where available – are often variations on burgers, sausages, fish and chips or pasta, and ice cream; some chefs will prepare special dishes.

In France, children generally get in free to museums, although the age varies from under 12s to under 18s; the permanent collections of national museums are free for under 26s; Nice's municipal museums are free for everyone.

Clothing

Cannes, Monaco and St-Tropez are the Riviera's dressiest places, although only the grandest restaurants and casinos require gentlemen to wear a jacket and tie *(tenue correcte)*. In general, think 'smart-casual' – avoid shorts for dining out at night and trainers if you want to get into exclusive nightclubs. A lot of attention is paid to accessories: the right sandals, sunglasses or bag can make all the difference. Try not to wander around the streets in swimwear; in Monaco it is formally forbidden and respectable attire is required for religious buildings.

Even in summer, a sweater, wrap or light jacket is useful for cooler evenings, and a waterproof coat or jacket will be needed from October to April.

Crime and Safety

Such a prosperous region inevitably attracts petty criminals, but incidents of violent crime against visitors are rare. Do not carry lots of cash, never

Niki de Saint-Phalle's Loch Ness Monster fountain outside the Théâtre National de Nice

leave valuables in your car, and look out for pickpockets, especially in crowds; in Nice, be careful of bags or watches snatched through open car windows when waiting at traffic lights. Any loss or theft should be reported immediately to the nearest *commissariat de police*.

Customs

As France is part of the EU, free exchange of non-duty-free goods for personal use is permitted between France and the UK and the Republic of Ireland. If you go to the very popular Friday street market in Ventimiglia (Ventimille in French) just across the border in Italy, be careful about buying counterfeit goods; customs checks are frequent at the Menton border post and you could be prosecuted.

For residents of non-EU countries, restrictions on bringing goods into France are as follows: 200 cigarettes or 50 cigars or 250g tobacco, 1 litre of spirits and 2 litres of wine. Non-EU residents can claim a refund *(détaxe)* of TVA (VAT) on certain goods, such as clothes, if they spend more than €175 in one shop on one day. Ask for a *bordereau de vente à l'exportation*, which should be stamped by customs on leaving and then posted back to the shop.

D

Disabled Travellers

Disabled access can be difficult in historic buildings or the stepped streets of old hill towns, but many of the south's recently renovated museums do have wheelchair access. All hotels built since 1978 should have at least one specially adapted bedroom, while public buildings constructed since 1978 should also be accessible. The Association des Paralysés de France (www. apf.asso.fr) produces an annual *Guide Vacances*. A Tourisme & Handicap classification (www.tourisme-handicaps. org) is gradually being introduced to show facilities accessible for visitors with physical, visual, hearing or learning difficulties.

E

Electricity

220-volt, 50-cycle AC is universal, generally with a three-pin plug. British visitors will need an adaptor *(adaptateur)*; American visitors will need a transformer *(transformateur)*.

Embassies and Consulates

Australia: (embassy) 4 rue Jean-Rey, 75015 Paris; tel: 01 40 50 33 00; www. france.embassy.gov.au.
Canada: (consulate) 35 avenue Montaigne, 75008 Paris; tel: 01 44 43 29 02; www.canadainternational.gc.ca.
Republic of Ireland: (embassy) 12 avenue Foch, 75116 Paris; tel: 01 44 17 67 00; www.embassyofireland.fr.
UK: (consulate) 24 avenue du Prado, 13006 Marseille; tel: 04 91 15 72 10; www.gov.uk.

Buying sunflowers on the Cours Saleya in Nice

US: (consulate) 7 avenue Gustave V, 06000 Nice; tel: 04 93 88 89 55; http://marseille.usconsulate.gov/nice.html

Emergencies

Ambulance: 15
Police: 17
Fire brigade *(sapeurs-pompiers)*: 18 (will also answer medical emergencies) Dial **112** from a mobile phone for all emergencies.

Etiquette

Madame/Mademoiselle and *Monsieur* are widely used in French. Unless you know someone well or are talking to children, use the formal *vous* rather than *tu* form. It is polite to shake hands when meeting someone. Do not kiss cheeks with someone you do not know, unless they propose to 'donne la bise'; a polite peck on either cheek. And note that topless bathing (very in during the 1980s and 1990s) has gone totally out of fashion.

G

Gay/Lesbian Issues

France is generally gay tolerant. Nice and Cannes have several gay bars and clubs; Coco Beach east of Nice's Vieux Port is a popular gay beach. *Nice Practical Guide* and *www Cannes*, published by the respective tourist offices, list gay and gay-friendly bars and hotels. There's a lively Gay Pride parade in July in Nice.

Green Issues

Despite the huge potential for solar energy, France has been slow to take it up, with general reliance on state-generated nuclear energy, and there are limitations on use of solar panels in picturesque listed villages. However, most towns have recycling schemes for glass and newspapers and many hotels try to promote environmental awareness by conserving water and encouraging guests not to change towels every day.

Air travel produces a huge amount of carbon dioxide and is a significant contributor to global warming. If you would like to offset the damage caused to the environment by your flight, a number of organisations can do this for you using online 'carbon calculators' that tell you how much you need to donate. In the UK visit www.climatecare.org or www.carbonneutral.com; in the US log on to www.climatefriendly.com or www.sustainabletravelinternational.org.

H

Health

Healthcare is generally of an extremely high standard in France and the Côte d'Azur has the highest concentration of specialist doctors in France outside Paris. There are no compulsory vaccinations or particular health risks. Tap water is safe to drink, unless marked *eau non potable*. However, be careful to avoid sunburn; wear a sunhat and avoid

St Tropez glitz

exposure to the powerful midday sun. Other potential hazards are mosquitoes (many people use plug-in anti-mosquito diffusers) and, in some years, invasions of jellyfish *(méduses)* in the sea.

EU nationals can use the French Social Security system, which refunds up to 70 percent of medical expenses. British nationals should obtain a European Health Insurance Card before leaving the UK (www.ehic.org.uk). If you are ill, your hotel can probably recommend an English-speaking doctor or dentist; make sure it is a *médecin conventionné* (affiliated to the social security system). You will get a prescription and a *feuille de soins* (statement of treatment), allowing you to claim back part of the cost upon your return.

Nationals of non-EU countries should take out travel and medical insurance before leaving home.

Pharmacies and Hospitals

Pharmacies (indicated by a green cross) can provide basic medicaments and deal with minor ailments. The name and address of duty chemists open on Sunday and at night is displayed in pharmacies; the police station or local papers will also have it. There is an all-night pharmacy in Nice at 7 rue Masséna.

24-hour casualty departments *(urgences)*. Centre Hospitalier Universitaire (CHU) St-Roch, 5 rue Piere Dévoluy, Nice; tel: 04 92 03 33 33. Centre Hospitalier Princesse Grace, 1 avenue Pasteur, Monaco; tel: +377-97 98 97 69.

Hours and Holidays

Banks. Most banks are open Mon–Fri 9am–noon and 2–5pm; some open Saturday morning and close on Monday.

Museums. Major ones usually open 10am–5 or 6pm (later in summer) and often close on Monday or Tuesday; smaller museums often close for lunch.

Restaurants. These usually serve noon–2 or 2.30pm, 7.30 or 8pm–9.30 or 10pm, and may close one or two days a week; cafés and brasseries often open from early morning until late.

Shops. Shops generally open Mon–Sat 9.30 or 10am–7pm; small shops often take a long lunch break, closing at noon and reopening at 3 or 4pm; bakeries usually open 8am–8pm and may open on Sunday, closing another day a week; some supermarkets open till 9 or 10pm.

Public Holidays

1 Jan Nouvel An – New Year's Day
Mar/Apr Lundi de Pâques – Easter Monday
1 May Fête du Travail – Labour Day
8 May Fête de la Victoire 1945 – VE Day
May Ascension
May/June Lundi de Pentecôte – Whit Monday
14 July Fête Nationale – Bastille Day
15 Aug Assomption – Assumption
1 Nov Toussaint – All Saints' Day
11 Nov Anniversaire de l'Armistice – Armistice Day
25 Dec Noël – Christmas

Baie de Garavan, Menton

Internet Facilities

Wi-fi is available in the majority of hotels (often but not always free) and there are also hotspots in numerous cafés; Cannes is gradually installing a free Wi-fi network 'Cannes sans fil'. Many hotels also have a computer with internet access in the lobby. Tourist offices should be able to supply addresses of internet cafés.

K

Kids

Nice's beach is pebbly, but some private concessions have sandpits and children's pools. Otherwise, Antibes, Bormes-les-Mimosas and Le Lavandou all have sandy beaches. Nice also has lots of small garden-square playgrounds in the New Town, plus the Parc Floral Phoenix (www.parc-phoenix.org). In Antibes, Marineland (www.marineland.fr) has animal shows and a waterpark, while there is an aquarium in Monaco's Musée Océanographique. Both Monaco and Cannes have firework displays in summer.

L

Language

The southern French accent draws out syllables and places extra emphasis on the ends of words or sentences. The usual nasal French 'en' ending becomes a hard 'ng' (*chien* sounds like *chieng*). In Vieux Nice you may see bilingual street names and hear Nissart, an old Occitan Provençal dialect that is experiencing a fashionable revival. French is the official language in Monaco, but Italian and English are also widely spoken; you may also come across Monégasque (an Italian dialect).

A list of useful words and phrases can be found in the Language chapter (see page 134).

Left Luggage

Since 9/11, security measures mean that only the largest train stations (Nice and Cannes) have left luggage facilities, with rather irregular hours. If you have an evening train or plane to catch, most hotels will store your luggage after checkout.

Lost Property

Lost property (*objets trouvés*) and lost passports should be reported to the police. The SNCF (French railways) has its own lost property system.

Police Nationale, 1 avenue Maréchal Foch, Nice; tel: 04 92 17 22 22.

SNCF, 1 rue Raoul Bosio, Nice; tel: 04 97 13 44 10.

Commissariat de Police, 1 avenue de Grasse, Cannes; tel: 04 93 06 22 22.

Direction de la Sûreté Publique, 9 rue Suffren Reymond, Monaco; tel: +377-93 15 30 15 (lost property, tel: +377-93 15 30 18).

Chillies at Nice's cours Saleya market

M

Maps

Hotel and tourist offices can usually supply a town street map *(un plan)*. For driving, a 1:200,000 or 1:250,000 scale road atlas or sheet map *(carte routière)* of Provence Côte d'Azur is useful. For serious hiking, buy 1:25,000 scale maps published by IGN.

Media

Newspapers. The British press is widely available in main cities and tourist destinations, as is *USA Today* and the Paris-based International New York Times. Alongside French national dailies *Le Monde, Le Figaro* and *Libération*, the two main local newspapers are *Nice Matin* and *Var Matin*. Look out also for glossy expat *magazine Riviera Reporter* (www.riviera-reporter.com), which can also be downloaded, and monthly newspaper *The Riviera News*.

Radio. State radio stations include France Info, France Inter and France Musiques. Commercial stations include news-oriented Europe 1 and RTL, music stations NRJ and Nostalgie. Monaco's Riviera Radio broadcasts local news, sport and weather in English; frequencies vary across the region.

TV. The main TV channels are TF1, France 2, France 3, M6 and Arte; many hotels also have numerous cable and satellite channels, often including CNN, BBC World and Sky News.

Money

Currency. France is part of the euro-zone. Banknotes are available in denominations of 500, 200, 100, 50, 20, 10 and 5 euros; avoid the largest denominations as many shops will not accept €200 and €500 notes. There are coins for 2 and 1 euros and for 50, 20, 10, 5, 2 and 1 cent.

Credit cards *(cartes de crédit)*. These are widely accepted, especially Visa and Mastercard. Note that there may be a minimum spending sum (generally €15).

Lost and stolen credit cards: American Express, tel: 01 47 77 70 00; Diners Club, tel: +44 1244 470910; Eurocard/Mastercard, tel: 0800 901 387; Visa, tel: 0800 901179.

Cash machines. ATMs are the simplest, and usually cheapest, way of obtaining cash in euros. They are plentiful in large cities, though may be scarce in rural areas.

Traveller's cheques. Traveller's cheques are rarely used; it is better to draw cash from a machine or use your credit card.

Tipping. A 10–15 per cent service charge is included in hotel and restaurant bills, so any further tip is optional, although rounding off bills with a few coins or small notes helps round off friendships with waiters, too. It is also in order to hand hotel porters, filling station attendants, etc, a coin or two for services.

P

Police

Theft should be reported to the Police Nationale in Nice (1 avenue Maréchal Foch, Nice; tel: 04 92 17 22 22) and Cannes or to the Gendarmerie in smaller towns and rural areas. Monaco has its own, highly visible, police force. Call 17 within France for police assistance.

Post

Post offices are indicated by a yellow 'La Poste' sign. When sending letters and small packages, it is often quicker to use the automatic stamp machines than to queue for service. *Tabacs* (tobacconists) also sell stamps. Letter boxes are yellow. It costs €0.61 to send a postcard or letter up to 20g within France, €0.83 to the EU and €0.98 to the rest of the world. Monaco stamps should be used to post letters from Monaco.

Nice's main post office, opposite the train station on avenue Thiers, is open Mon–Fri 8am–7pm and Sat 8am–12.30pm; smaller post offices usually open Mon–Fri 9am–noon and 2–5pm, Sat 9am–noon.

R

Religion

The French Republic has officially been a lay state since the French Revolution and does not have an established religion; however, the church calendar determines most public holidays and the majority of the population is nominally Roman Catholic, with substantial minority Protestant, Muslim and Jewish communities. Non-Catholic services are called *cultes*; Protestant churches are known as *temples*. Roman Catholicism is the established religion in Monaco.

There are Anglican churches with regular services in English in Nice, Cannes, Menton, Monaco and Vence.

S

Smoking

Smoking is prohibited in all state-owned buildings and public places, including post offices, stations, cinemas and museums, and on public transport. Since 1 January 2008 this has been extended to restaurants, bars, cafés, discothèques and casinos, except in specially ventilated, sealed-off *fumoirs* or outside on café terraces; smoking is banned in the public areas of hotels, but not in hotel bedrooms unless they are designated non-smoking rooms.

T

Telephones

France uses a 10-digit telephone-number system. Numbers on the French Riviera begin with 04. Mobile

Looking out from La Croisette

phones start with 06; special-rate numbers varying from freephone 0800 to premium-rate 0892 start with 08. Directory enquiries are available from various providers, including 118000, 118712 and 118218.

When dialling France from abroad, dial the French country code 33 and omit the 0 at the start of the 10-digit number. To dial overseas from France, dial 00, followed by the country code (UK: 44; Canada and US: 1; Australia: 61; Monaco: 377) and then the number, usually omitting the initial zero.

Many public telephones only accept *télécartes* (phone cards), available from post offices and tobacconists. A surcharge will usually be added for calls made from your hotel room.

Mobile (cell) phones. Check with your network provider in your own country if your phone will work in France (UK phones do). If so, check that your phone is set up for international roaming and buy bundles of minutes to use in Europe to keep costs down. For longer stays you can buy a French SIM card for your own phone or a pay-as-you-go (sans abonnement) mobile phone from Orange (www.orange.fr), SFR (www.sfr.fr) or Bouygues Telecom (www.bouyguestelecom.fr), all of whom have shops on the high street. If you are using a British-based mobile *(portable)* in France, dial as if you are a local subscriber. To call from one British phone to another, use the international code even if you are both in France.

Time Zones

France is one hour ahead of GMT and clocks go forward one hour between March and October.

Toilets

There are free toilets in museums and department stores. If using a toilet in a café, it is polite to order at least a coffee at the bar.

Tourist Information

Tourist offices *(offices de tourisme)* can provide maps and information on hotels, restaurants, sightseeing, festivals and tours and may have hotel reservation and ticket sales services. See also the tourist board websites for the Alpes-Maritimes (www.cotedazur-tourisme.com), the Var (www.visitvar.fr) and Paca regional tourist board (www.decouverte-paca.fr).

Nice: 5 promenade des Anglais, tel: 08 92 70 74 07; www.nicetourisme.com; branches at Nice train station (avenue Thiers) and Aéroport Nice Côte d'Azur (T1).

Antibes: 42 avenue Robert Soleau; tel: 04 22 10 60 10; www.antibes-juanles pins.com.

Cannes: Palais des Festivals, La Croisette; tel: 04 92 99 84 22; www.cannes-destination.fr.

Grasse:Place de la Buanderie; tel: 04 93 36 66 66; www.grasse.fr.

Menton: Palais de l'Europe, 8 avenue Boyer; tel: 04 92 41 76 76; www.

Nice train station

tourisme-menton.fr.

Monaco: 2a boulevard des Moulins, Monte Carlo; tel: +377-92 16 61 16; www.visitmonaco.com.

St-Tropez: quai Jean Jaurès; tel: 08 92 68 48 28; www.ot-saint-tropez.com.

Vence: 8 place du Grand Jardin; tel: 04 93 58 06 38; www.vence-tourisme. com.

Transport

Arrival by Air

Aéroport Nice-Côte d'Azur (tel: 08 20 42 33 33; www.nice.aeroport.fr), on the western edge of Nice, is France's second busiest airport. Flights leave from two terminals, with scheduled connections from all major European cities, North Africa and some American cities.

RCA buses (www.rca.tm.fr) depart from Nice airport for main destinations along the coast: line 99 (T1 and T2) serve Nice railway station *(gare SNCF)*; lines 110 Aéroport-Monte-Carlo-Menton Express and 210 Aéroport-Cannes Express are express services along the motorway. Buy tickets before boarding at the desks signposted 'Car Park/Bus Cash' inside the terminals. A free shuttle runs between the terminals and the car parks.

A typical taxi fare to the centre of Nice would be €23–33, Cannes €70–87 and Monaco €72–92.

Heli Air Monaco (tel: +377-92 05 00 50; www.heliairmonaco.com) runs scheduled helicopter services between Nice airport and Monaco that take 6 minutes and are not necessarily much more expensive than a taxi (approximately €135).

The small **Aéroport Toulon-Hyères** (tel: 08 25 01 83 87; www.toulon-hyeres. aeroport.fr) is located in Hyères and served by Ryanair flights from London Stansted and London City.

Arrival by Rail

From the UK, Eurostar trains (tel: 08432 186 186; www.eurostar.co.uk) run from London St Pancras to Lille and Paris Gare du Nord. Services for the South depart from Paris Gare de Lyon. The high-speed TGV reaches Nice in 6 hours; some trains also stop at St-Raphaël (for boats to St-Tropez), Cannes, Antibes, Monaco and Menton.

In the UK, tickets can be booked at Voyages -SNCF Travel Centre (193 Piccadilly, London, W1J 9EU, tel: 0844 848 5848) or online (www.voyages-sncf. com). In the US, call 1-800-622-8600 or visit www.raileurope.com/us.

By motor-rail. The SNCF operates a direct service from Paris to Nice (tel: 0844 848 3339, www.voyages-sncf. com) called AutoTrain.

Driving

To Nice from the UK by car (via Paris or Rheims) with Eurotunnel from Folkestone or car ferry from Dover to Calais, is around 1,240km (770 miles). To bring a car into France you will need a valid driving licence, your car registra-

Col du Canadel in the Massif des Maures

tion papers, insurance coverage and a set of spare bulbs. A red warning triangle and a fluorescent safety waistcoat are obligatory in case of breakdown. You must also carry two breathalysers with an 'NF' number. If you are driving your own car it must have a GB sticker. Drivers and all passengers (back and front) are required by law to wear seat belts. Children under 10 may not travel in the front, except in appropriate baby seats with the air bag disconnected.

Driving regulations. Drive on the right, pass on the left. In built-up areas, give priority to vehicles coming from the right unless indicated by road markings. The speed limit is 130km/h (80mph) on *autoroutes* (motorways); 110km/h (70mph) on dual carriageways; 90km/h (55mph) on other country roads; and 50km/h (30mph) in built-up areas (30km/h (20mph) in some residential districts). Speed limits are reduced in wet weather. There are speed radars installed on some roads. Note that most *autoroutes* are toll roads *(péages).*

Roads can get very clogged up in summer especially on Saturdays and around the 14 July and 15 August public holidays. You can spend as much time getting to the beach as you spend on it. Try to avoid weekends, mid- to late mornings (when everyone's going to the beach), and late afternoons (when everyone's going home from the beach). There is often less traffic at lunchtime, and on Sunday, when lorries are not allowed to travel.

Motorways *(autoroutes)* are designated 'A' roads, National Highways *(routes nationales)* 'N' or 'RN' roads. Local roads are known as 'D' routes and very small 'C' communal roads. Note that many roads have recently been renumbered, as former N roads have come under local control and have been renumbered as D routes.

Parking in the main resorts is often costly; parking meters have been replaced by *horodateurs,* (pay-and-display machines), which take coins and/or special parking cards that can be bought at a tobacconist *(tabac).*

British, US, Canadian and Australian licences are all valid in France. You should always carry your vehicle's registration document and valid insurance. Additional insurance cover, in some cases including a 'home-return' service, is offered by a number of organisations, including the AA (tel: 0800 072 3279; www.theaa.com) and Aria-Assistance (tel: 0844 338 5533; www.aria-assistance.co.uk).

Car rental. The major car-rental companies all have branches at Nice airport; most also have branches in Nice (around the train station), Cannes and Monaco. To rent a car, you must have a driving licence (held for at least one year) and a passport. The minimum age is 20–23. Third-party insurance is compulsory. Major car-hire companies include:

Avis: tel: 0820 61 16 32; www.avis. com; **Budget:** tel: 08 25 00 35 64;

Antibes yachts

www.budget.com; **Europcar:** tel: 08 25 358 358; www.europcar.com; **Hertz:** tel: 0825 34 23 43; www.hertz-europe.com.

Car Ferry Operators

The following companies operate across the English Channel:

Brittany Ferries sails from Portsmouth to Caen, Cherbourg, Le Havre and St-Malo; from Plymouth to Roscoff; from Cork to Roscoff; and from Poole to Cherbourg. Tel: 0871 244 0744 (UK); 0825 828 828 (France); 021 4277 801 (Ireland); www.brittany-ferries.com

DFDS Seaways sails from Dover to Dunkerque and Calais; from Newhaven to Dieppe; and from Portsmouth to Le Havre. Tel: 0871 574 7235 (UK); +44 208 127 8303 (France); www.dfdsseaways.co.uk

MyFerryLink sails from Dover to Calais. Tel: 0844 2482 100 (UK); +44 845 313 3380 (France); www.myferrylink.com.

P&O sails from Dover to Calais in 90 minutes. Tel: 08716 64 64 64 (UK); 03 66 74 03 25 (France); www.poferries.com

Eurotunnel

Eurotunnel carries cars and their passengers from Folkestone to Calais on a simple drive-on-drive-off train system (journey time 35 minutes). Payment is made at toll booths (which accept cash, cheques or credit cards). For the best prices and to avoid queues, it is best to book ahead (tel: 08443 35 35 35 (UK); 0810 630 304 (France); www.eurotunnel.com).

Public Transport

Bus and tram. Nice has a comprehensive network of urban bus routes and a tramway run by Lignes d'Azur (www.lignesdazur.com), plus five night bus routes (every 30 min, 9.10pm–1.10am). Single journeys have a flat rate of €1.50 (valid for 74 minutes and including one transfer), which can be bought on the bus; the same tickets can be used on buses and trams (but not airport express buses); a one-day pass, including airport buses, costs €5.

Regional bus services between Nice, Cannes and Menton are run by RCA (Rapides Côte d'Azur, www.rca.tm.fr). Buses in the Var are run by Sodetrav (www.sodetrav.fr).

Train. There are frequent TER regional trains along the coast, stopping at most towns between Cannes and Menton, with a branch line inland from Cannes to Grasse (see www.ter-sncf.com/Paca for schedules).

Bicycle. Like most major French cities, Nice offers a municipal bike hire scheme (www.velobleu.org), with 90 stations spread out around the city. Bikes can also be hired at Holiday Bikes (www.holiday-bikes.com), which has branches in Nice and several other towns. Two scenic mountain lines depart from Nice: the **Roya Valley line** aka the 'Train des Merveilles' runs from Nice to Tende through the Peil-

Nice tram

lon and Roya-Bévéra valleys. The privately operated **Train des Pignes** (tel: 04 97 03 80 80; www.trainprovence. com) has four return journeys from Nice Gare de Provence that run up the Var valley to Digne les Bains. Vintage steam trains run on Sundays from May to October.

Boat. A good way to avoid traffic jams on the French Riviera is to take a boat to your destination. Trans Côte d'Azur (www.trans-cote-azur.com) runs day trips from Nice and Cannes to Monaco and St-Tropez. Les Bateaux de St-Raphaël (tel: 04 94 95 17 46, www. bateauxsaintraphael.com) run day trips from St-Raphaël to St-Tropez while Les Bateaux Verts (tel: 04 94 49 29 39, www.bateauxverts.com) link St-Tropez with Cogolin, Port Grimaud, Ste-Maxime and Les Issambres; they also organise day trips to Cannes from St-Tropez, Ste-Maxime and Les Issambres.

Taxis

Nice's taxis are notoriously expensive; try Central Taxi Riviera (tel: 04 93 13 78 78; www.taxis-nice.fr). Allo Taxi cover Cannes (tel: 08 90 71 22 27; www. allo-taxi-cannes.com) and Monaco (tel: +377-93 15 01 01; www.taximonaco-prestige.com).

V

Visas and Passports

British visitors need only a passport to enter France, as do nationals of other EU countries and Switzerland. US citizens do not need a visa for stays of up to 90 days. Other nationalities should check with the French Embassy in their country for entry requirements.

W

Websites

As well as tourist offices try the following for useful information:

www.beyond.fr – English-language for Provence and the Côte d'Azur

www.cannes.com – Cannes' municipal website

www.cote.azur.fr – directory of hotels, rentals and activities

www.monte-carlo.mc – official guide to the principality

www.nice.fr – Nice's municipal website

www.nicerendezvous.com – Nice past and present

http://riviera.angloinfo.com – practical directory of English-language services, events and culture

Women Travellers

Women should have no problem travelling on the French Riviera, although the usual safety precautions should be taken when walking around late at night. France has one of Europe's highest proportions of women who work and it is totally acceptable for women to go alone to cafés and restaurants (however as a solo diner don't be surprised if you get refused a table during busy periods).

LANGUAGE

In general, if you attempt to communicate in French, the fact that you have made an effort is likely to break the ice and win favour with Parisians.

General

yes *oui*
no *non*
please *s'il vous plaît*
thank you (very much) *merci (beaucoup)*
you're welcome *de rien*
excuse me *excusez-moi*
hello *bonjour*
hi/bye *salut*
OK *d'accord*
goodbye *au revoir*
good evening *bonsoir*
How much is it? *C'est combien?*
What is your name? *Comment vous appelez-vous?*
My name is... *Je m'appelle...*
Do you speak English? *Parlez-vous anglais?*
I am English/American *Je suis anglais(e)/américain(e)*
I don't understand *Je ne comprends pas*
Please speak more slowly *Parlez plus lentement, s'il vous plaît*
Can you help me? *Pouvez-vous m'aider?*
I'm looking for... *Je cherche...*
Where is...? *Où est...?*
I'm sorry *Excusez-moi/Pardon*
I don't know *Je ne sais pas*
See you soon *A bientôt*
When? *Quand?*

What time is it? *Quelle heure est-il?*
here *ici*
there *là*
left *gauche*
right *droite*
straight on *tout droit*
far *loin*
near *près d'ici*
opposite *en face*
beside *à côté de*
today *aujourd'hui*
yesterday *hier*
tomorrow *demain*
now *maintenant*
later *plus tard*
this morning *ce matin*
this afternoon *cet après-midi*
this evening *ce soir*

Getting around

I want to get off at... *Je voudrais descendre à...*
Which line do I take for...? *Quelle ligne dois-je prendre pour...?*
Validate your ticket *Compostez votre billet*
airport *l'aéroport*
railway station *la gare*
bus station *la gare routière*
metro stop *la station de Métro*
bus *l'autobus, le car*
bus stop *l'arrêt*
platform *le quai*
ticket *le billet*
return ticket *aller-retour*

Spoilt for choice

Emergencies

Help! *Au secours!*
Stop! *Arrêtez!*
Where is the nearest telephone? *Où est le téléphone le plus proche?*
Where is the nearest hospital? *Où est l'hôpital le plus proche?*
I am sick *Je suis malade*
I have lost my passport/purse *J'ai perdu mon passeport/porte-monnaie*

Shopping

I'd like to buy *Je voudrais acheter*
How much is it? *C'est combien?*
Do you take credit cards? *Est-ce que vous acceptez les cartes de crédit?*
I'm just looking *Je regarde seulement*
size (clothes) *la taille*
size (shoes) *la pointure*
receipt *le reçu*

Sightseeing

tourist information office *l'office du tourisme*
free *gratuit*
open *ouvert*
closed *fermé*
every day *tous les jours*
to book *réserver*
town map *le plan*
road map *la carte*

Dining out

breakfast *le petit-déjeuner*
lunch *le déjeuner*
dinner *le dîner*
meal *le repas*
first course *l'entrée*

main course *le plat principal*
drink included *boisson comprise*
wine list *la carte des vins*
the bill *l'addition*
I am a vegetarian *Je suis végétarien(ne)*
I'd like to order *Je voudrais commander*
service included *service compris*

Online communications

Where's an internet cafe? *Où y-a-t-il un cyber café?*
Does it have wireless internet? *Est-ce qu'il a la connexion WiFi?*
What is the WiFi password? *Quel est le mot de passe du WiFi?*
Is the WiFi free? *Est-ce que le WiFi est gratuit?*
Do you have bluetooth? *Avez-vous Bluetooth?*
Can I...? *Puis-je...?*
...access the internet *accéder à Internet*
...check my e-mail *consulter mes mails*
...print *imprimer*
...access Skype? *accéder à Skype?*
How much per half hour/hour? *Combien coûte la demi-heure/l'heure?*

Social Media

Are you on Facebook/Twitter? *Etes-vous sur Facebook/Twitter?*
What's your user name? *Quel est votre nom d'utilisateur ?*
I'll add you as a friend. *Je vous ajouterai comme ami.*
I'll put the pictures on Facebook/Twitter. *Je mettrai les photos sur Facebook/Twitter.*

Michael Caine and Steve Martin in Dirty Rotten Scoundrels

BOOKS AND FILM

Writers and filmmakers have long been attracted to the French Riviera. Originally British and American scribes including D H Lawrence and Katherine Mansfield came here to try and cure or ease their tuberculosis while directors, like so many artists, were drawn to the light and the landscape.

The earliest account of the area was penned by Scottish writer Tobias Smollett in his 1766 book *Travels though France and Italy* following a winter stay in Nice. Since then, dozens of authors have written about the French Riviera. This part of France continues to provide an appealing backdrop for novels, especially the 'chick-lit' variety.

In the 1920s Nice became the centre of European film making after the Victorine film studios were bought by Hollywood director Rex Ingram. The *Nouvelle Vague* (New Wave) directors of the 1950s and 60s also filmed in Nice: François Truffaut's *La nuit américaine* (*American Night*, 1972) was partly shot at the Victorine Studios and Jacques Demy's *La Baie des Anges* (*Bay of Angels*, 1962) was set in the city. Meanwhile, Roger Vadim not only created a star out of Brigitte Bardot with his 1956 offering *Et Dieu créa la femme* (*And God Created Woman*) but out of its location, Saint Tropez, too. The coast continues to provide an enticing prospect for both foreign and French films such as the hit 2010 offering *L'Arnacoeur* (*Heartbreaker*) starring Vanessa Paradis.

Books

Non-Fiction

Côte d'Azur: Inventing the French Riviera by Mary Blume. Excellent account of emigré Riviera.

The Discovery of France by Graham Robb. Quirky anecdotes tell the history of France.

France on the Brink: A Great Civilization Faces the New Century by Jonathan Fenby. Controversial and witty account of French politics and life.

The French by Theodore Zeldin. Irreverent, penetrating analysis of the French character. Although written in the 1980s, it has become a classic.

The French Riviera: A Literary Guide for Travellers by Ted Jones. Writers in the South of France.

The Identity of France by Fernand Braudel. Unputdownable analysis, weaving major events with everyday life, by one of France's best historians.

The Most Beautiful Villages of Provence by Michael Jacobs and Hugh Palmer. Lovely photos of Provençal villages.

Operation Dragoon: The Invasion of Southern France 1944 by Anthony Tucker-Jones. Account of the Allied landings.

Cary Grant and other bronzed bodies in To Catch a Thief

Picasso: A Biography by Patrick O'Brian. The artist's life, including his time in the South of France.

Fiction

The Mystery of the Blue Train by Agatha Christie. A murder takes place on a train bound for the French Riviera.

Bonjour Tristesse by Françoise Sagan. The story of a teenager and her father, living the hedonistic Riviera life.

Perfume by Patrick Süskind. Sinister but gripping tale of an 18th-century Grasse perfumier.

The Rock Pool by Cyril Connolly. Satirical novel set in 1930s Riviera.

Loser Takes All by Graham Greene. A young English couple encounter problems when the go on honeymoon to Monaco.

Super-Cannes by J G Ballard. A futuristic thriller set in a gated business park on the Riviera, loosely inspired by Sophia-Antipolis.

Tender is the Night by F. Scott Fitzgerald. Wealth and decadence on the Riviera.

Hotel Paradise by Carol Drinkwater. A songwriter revisits a French Riviera hotel after 12 years.

Film

To Catch A Thief (1955). Directed by Alfred Hitchcock and starring Grace Kelly and Cary Grant. A reformed jewel thief helps catch a current jewel thief working on the French Riviera.

Monte Carlo or Bust (1969). Starring Tony Curtis and Peter Cook, this comedy is based on the Monte Carlo Rally.

The Day of the Jackal (1973). Nice and Grasse feature in this film about an assassination attempt on General de Gaulle by Edward Fox's 'Jackal'.

The Return of the Pink Panther (1974). Some scenes take place in Nice in the third film featuring Peter Sellers as the hapless detective.

Never Say Never Again (1983). Antibes and Beaulieu-sur-Mer feature in the last James Bond film to star Sir Sean Connery.

Dirty Rotten Scoundrels (1988). Sir Michael Caine and Steve Martin star in this comedy about conmen trying to outwit each other on the French Riviera.

French Kiss (1995). Some scenes were shot in Cannes in this comedy about two reluctant lovers starring Meg Ryan and Kevin Kline.

Golden Eye (1995). Filming took place in several locations on the French Riviera in the second James Bond film to feature Pierce Brosnan.

Ronin (1998). Look out for the car chase around Vieux Nice in this spy thriller starring Robert de Niro and Jean Reno.

Ocean's 12 (2004). Cap Martin and Monaco star briefly alongside George Clooney and Brad Pitt.

Mr Bean's Holiday (2007). Rowan Atkinson's hopeless anti-hero goes to Cannes Film Festival.

Grace of Monaco (2014). Starring Nicole Kidman, this film about Princess Grace was partly shot in Monaco and Menton.

ABOUT THIS BOOK

This *Explore Guide* has been produced by the editors of Insight Guides, whose books have set the standard for visual travel guides since 1970. With top-quality photography and authoritative recommendations, these guidebooks bring you the very best routes and itineraries in the world's most exciting destinations.

BEST ROUTES

The routes in the book provide something to suit all budgets, tastes and trip lengths. As well as covering the destination's many classic attractions, the itineraries also track lesser-known sights. The routes embrace a range of interests, so whether you are an art fan, a gourmet, a history buff or have kids to entertain, you will find an option to suit.

We recommend reading the whole of a route before setting out. This should help you to familiarise yourself with it and enable you to plan where to stop for refreshments – options are shown in the 'Food and Drink' box at the end of each tour.

For our pick of the tours by theme, consult Recommended Routes for… (see pages 4–5).

INTRODUCTION

The routes are set in context by this introductory section, giving an overview of the destination to set the scene, plus background information on food and drink, shopping and more, while a succinct history timeline highlights the key events over the centuries.

DIRECTORY

Also supporting the routes is a Directory chapter, with a clearly organised A–Z of practical information, our pick of where to stay while you are there and select restaurant listings; these eateries complement the more low-key cafés and restaurants that feature within the routes and are intended to offer a wider choice for evening dining. Also included here are some nightlife listings, plus a handy language guide and our recommendations for books and films about the destination.

ABOUT THE AUTHOR

Victoria Trott is a passionate Francophile who has updated several guidebooks on France for Insight Guides and has travelled extensively in the country. She has also contributed to magazines *Living France*, *France Magazine* and *French Entrée*.

CONTACT THE EDITORS

We hope you find this Explore Guide useful, interesting and a pleasure to read. If you have any questions or feedback on the text, pictures or maps, please do let us know. If you have noticed any errors or outdated facts, or have suggestions for places to include on the routes, we would be delighted to hear from you. Please drop us an email at insight@apaguide.co.uk. Thanks!

CREDITS

Explore Nice and the French Riviera
Contributors: Natasha Edwards,
Victoria Trott
Commissioning Editor: Carine Tracanelli
Picture Editor: Tom Smyth
Map Production: original cartography
Berndtson & Berndtson, updated by Apa
Cartography Department
Production: Rebeka Davies

Photo credits: 123RF 41, 42, 51, 131;
Alamy 136, 137; Bigstock 87; Design Hotels
106, 107; Fotolia 8, 85, 92/93, 95; Getty Images 2/3T, 6/7T, 24, 25, 90; Hi Hotel 96MR;
iStock 1, 2MR, 2ML, 4TL, 5M, 9, 12/13, 13L,
26ML, 26MC, 26MR, 26ML, 26MC, 26MR,
26/27T, 31, 32/33, 33L, 34, 35, 36, 37, 44,
48, 52/53, 58, 61L, 64/65, 66/67, 67L, 68,
72, 73, 74, 78/79, 86, 88, 130, 132, 133,
134, 135; Kube Hotels 108/109; La Bastide
Saint-Antoine 96ML, 116, 116/117, 117L;
Leonardo 96MC, 96ML, 96/97T, 98, 99,
100/101, 102, 103, 104, 104/105, 105L,
110/111, 112/113, 118, 118/119, 119L;
Les Ballets de Monte Carlo 20/21; Library
of Congress 6MC; Lucien Barrière Hôtels
& Casinos 2MC, 96MC, 120, 121; Ming
Tang-Evans/Apa Publications 6ML; Mirazur
96MR, 114, 115; Myrabella 70/71; Nicolas
Sartore/Office de Tourisme Menton 6MR,
22; Office de Tourisme Menton 6MC, 23; OTC
Nice 21L; Paul Downey 66; Sylvaine Poitau/
Apa Publications 2ML, 2MR, 4MC, 4ML,
4BC, 5T, 5MR, 5MR, 6ML, 6MR, 10, 11, 12,
14, 15, 16, 17, 18, 18/19, 19L, 20, 28,
29, 30, 32, 38, 38/39, 39L, 40, 43, 45, 46,
46/47, 47L, 49, 50, 54, 55, 56, 57, 59, 60,
60/61, 62, 63, 69, 75, 76, 77, 80, 81, 82,
83, 84, 91, 122, 123, 124, 126, 127, 128,
129; Wadey James/Apa Publications 2MC,
88/89, 89L, 94, 125
Cover credits: balcony, *Getty Images* **Front
Cover BL:** Villefranche, *Dreamstime* **Back
Cover: (Left)** Negresco Hotel *iStock* **(Right):**
chillies & garlic, Sylvaine Poitau/Apa
Publications

DISTRIBUTION

INDEX

MAP LEGEND

● Start of tour

→ Tour & route direction

❶ Recommended sight

❷ Recommended restaurant/café

★ Place of interest

❶ Tourist information

1 Statue/monument

✉ Main post office

🚌 Main bus station

☼ Viewpoint

Park

Important building

Hotel

Transport hub

Market/store

Pedestrian area

Urban area